ALONG COMES GOD

MIRACLES IN EVERYDAY LIFE

GEORGE R. SLATER

ALONG COMES GOD
Miracles in Everyday Life

©2011 George R. Slater

Printed in the United States of America

ISBN: 978-1-935507-57-4

Cover Design & Page Layout by Dena Hynes of Dena Hynes Design

AMBASSADOR INTERNATIONAL
Emerald House
427 Wade Hampton Blvd
Greenville, SC 29609, USA
www.ambassador-international.com

AMBASSADOR BOOKS
The Mount
2 Woodstock Link
Belfast, BT6 8DD, Northern Ireland, UK
www.ambassador-international.com
The colophon is a trademark of Ambassador

To Leonard Griffith, messenger, mentor and friend,
in deepest gratitude.

"...wonderful, almost unbelievable, stories....profoundly changed lives....George Slater is a skilled story teller who takes us into the heart of people's struggles and triumphs. Every reader will relate....Don't miss this hopeful and inspiring book."

-DR. MERLE R. JORDAN

Emeritus Professor of Pastoral Psychology, Boston University School of Theology, and author of "Reclaiming Your Story: Family History and Spiritual Growth."

"George Slater has mined the rich experiences of people who have miraculously encountered God in life-changing ways. Their inspiring stories contain nuggets of timeless truth ....Along Comes God is a delightful read that will lift your spirit ... "

-DR. KENNETH N. BROWN

Executive Director, Hope for Families, Adoption and Counseling Services, Ft. Pierce, Florida.

TABLE OF CONTENTS

INTRODUCTION

Come with me into a world of unexpected goodness and wonderfully gracious outcomes—amazing coincidences, narrow escapes, life-changing encounters, answered prayers, faith healings, and providential dreams. An on-duty fireman narrowly escapes death when terrorists crash an airbus into the Pentagon. A chiropractor almost dies climbing Mount Kilimanjaro except for a German cardiologist and his nurse wife who happen to be passing at the critical moment. A frantic housewife recovers her wedding ring through prayer. An electronics sales manager is delayed in rush hour traffic and misses his flight which crashes shortly after takeoff, killing all on board. These are just a few samples of the stories that follow.

The people are real. The stories are true. Their experiences are unique. All of them share one thing in common, however: each person was aware of an intervention in her or his life—an intervention that brought benefit, usually unexpectedly and without their planning. Some power, or Someone, was there for them.

Whether you are a believer in God or not, you will recognize the exceptional nature of these occurrences and see them as either the operation of rare chance or the working of a mind and purpose greater than our own. I personally believe that there are no accidents in life, that coincidence is one expression of God at work, and that everything is ultimately from God and conforms to God's good nature and will. Christians might use the words of

St. Paul to explain it: "We know that in all things God works for the good of those who love him, who have been called according to his purpose" (Romans 8:28 NIV).

These are very personal stories. A few are from my own experience, but most are from the lives of others. They emerged casually from conversations with friends and acquaintances or from chance meetings with strangers. I did not go looking for them; they found me. I have merely collected and organized them. For the most part they express the person's core experience—a pivotal point or essential understanding of their life, even their survival. Only a few could be called "blue sky" or utopian stories. The most moving of these accounts relate the magnificent responses people made from the depths of suffering and tragedy: The man whose son was killed and grandson maimed for life in an auto crash yet who not only forgave the driver but turned his grief into mission work among the Haitian people. The eight-year-old Vietnamese girl who incredibly provided for her younger brother and sister for two years by panning for gold and scratching a vegetable garden out of the jungle. The flight attendant who, driven to despair by her abusive marriage and divorce and preparing to throw herself from a Chicago high-rise, heard Jesus calling her and was saved. Seldom do we have the privilege of seeing into the intimate lives of others to this depth, to hear what actually happened to them and to know their thoughts and feelings. Wherever possible the story is told in their own words. In some cases, I have disguised personal identity to preserve their privacy, and **an asterisk will indicate the use of a pseudonym.** I want to thank each one who has trusted me with his or her story and for making it available to strengthen and encourage others in their faith.

Don Cherry's story of faith arrived just as this manuscript was going to the publisher. I have given his story a place of its own at the beginning. Here this internationally famous hockey coach and TV celebrity tells how he'd been a washed-up player at thirty-six and a hopeless failure who couldn't get work, and how the comeback of his life began there on his knees in prayer.

If your experience is like mine, God seems to act just off camera—just beyond the corner of your eye—like a movie director who is prompting, improvising, and moving actors in and out of scenes all while the cameras are rolling. The effects of God's actions are evident, though God is well hidden.

When something this good occurs, you want to tell others so that they will be encouraged too. At the same time you may hesitate because the goodness in the stories is in such sharp contrast to the terrible tragedies and unrelieved sufferings so many people experience. It may seem insensitive, even cruel, to focus on stories of divine blessing as part of the same world. The very nature of reality, of good and evil, is up for debate. However, the fact that such matters are difficult, even impossible, to understand is no reason to stifle the wonder of what these people experienced. I am convinced that their stories show the activity and presence of God here and now in human lives. They inspire us with evidence that God knows and cares for each of us. What happened to them could happen to us.

After Captain Chesley "Sully" Sullenberger crash-landed US Airways Flight 1549 safely in the Hudson River on January 15, 2009, saving all 155 persons aboard, he was asked how he felt about being called a hero. He answered that in the days immediately following the landing he had struggled with the idea. Neither did he feel comfortable accepting the title, nor did he want to deny the gratitude of those whose lives he had saved. Finally he resolved the matter by concluding, "Something about this episode has captured people's imagination. I think they want good news. I think they want to feel hopeful again. And if I can help in that way, I will."[1]

Like Captain Sullenberger, I believe people want good news. There is no end to stories of tragedy and the works of evil. All the more do we need to hear when good things happen and the hand of a loving God is seen in action. I invite you to take these wonderful stories to your heart. May they be a source of hope for you.

---

1. 60 Minutes Interview, February 8, 2009.

DON CHERRY'S COMEBACK

The envelope was large and white with my name and address scrawled across it in heavy black handwriting, with a flourish underneath for emphasis. Inside were fourteen handwritten pages. At the top of the first page were these words: "George, I would like your readers to see this. Don Cherry."

Two months earlier I had written to him. I had seen a story about him some years before and asked him for permission to include a personal part of his story in this book.[2] Those fourteen pages were his answer.

Don Cherry is known for "rock 'em sock 'em" hockey. He rose from being an unemployed, unremarkable player to making banner headlines as head coach of the Boston Bruins. In 1975–1976 he won the Jack Adams Award as National Hockey League Coach of the Year. The two following years he led the Bruins to the Stanley Cup finals. He was the toast of Beantown. In 1979, in the seventh game of the semifinals with his team up one goal and less than two minutes to go, it appeared his Bruins would go into the finals. Through a coaching error the game was tied, and they lost in overtime. Don was fired.

Two years later, there was some consolation in being chosen head coach of Canada's team in the 1981 World Championship in Stockholm, Sweden. But his coaching career was over.

---

2. Terry O'Neill, "Don Cherry 'Great Canadian Loudmouth,'" *Western Standard,* February 14, 2005.

Unstoppable, he launched himself into orbit as a star hockey commentator on major media, first in Canada and then the U.S., a hugely successful career which continues to this day.

He's been called hockey's biggest personality. In 2004, his Canadian fans voted him one of the "ten greatest Canadians." They say you either love him or hate him. His outspoken comments, flamboyant style, and politically incorrect opinions leave people no middle ground. If you're a hockey fan, you've seen him on TV and heard him on radio. You've cheered or jeered his rants and pomp; you know of his fierce Canadian patriotism and his legendary marriage to Rose, the light of his life. You may even know his softer side—his tribute following her death in 1997 in establishing the Rose Cherry Homes for Kids. But did you know of his faith in the Lord and how his amazing comeback in hockey was an answer to prayer? Here in his own words is Don Cherry's story of faith.[3]

I played professional hockey for sixteen years. We were like gypsies. Rose and I and the kids moved fifty-three times. I won't go into all the cities I played in. I will say that I played in every professional league that existed—but I only played one game in the N.H.L. But build one Bridge, you're a Bridge-Builder.

I was sailing along having fun, not thinking of the future. Finally the day came when I retired. I had a good construction job; the jackhammer was my specialty. Strong back, weak mind. One day, to my regret, I was laid off. I was in trouble. Like a fool, I'd quit school in Grade 10 and I had no trade to speak of—

3. For other stories by Don Cherry, see his latest book, *Don Cherry's Hockey Stories Part 2* (Doubleday Canada, 2010).

a jackhammer specialist is not in demand. I tried everything to get a job. I even went to construction sites and to the foreman and asked for work. It was so embarrassing and humiliating to come back to the car with Rose and the kids and shake my head.

Finally, after trying everywhere—I would have swept floors—I got a job painting at $2.00 an hour. People on welfare were getting better money, and like a fool I wouldn't accept unemployment money. A car company thought to cash in on my so-called fame as Captain of the Rochester Americans and hired me as a car salesman. I established myself as the worst car salesman in the world. When a customer said, "All you car salesmen are alike," I nailed him against the wall. I knew I wasn't cut out to be a car salesman, but my family had to eat. So I kept doing my best, but I was feeling depressed.

I couldn't seem to do anything right. I was a failure. It was all so sad—a failure at 36 years old. Nothing to look forward to in life. "Why, oh why, did I quit school and not get a trade?" It was a black time in my life.

One afternoon I lay down in bed staring at the ceiling, thinking of the mess I'd made of my life. Suddenly something seemed to tell me to get on my knees and ask the Lord to help, which I did. I prayed, "Lord, is this it? What am I going to do? I can't get a job. My life is just one big failure. I am embarrassed to look my wife and kids in the eye."

Now I know a lot of people are not going to believe this, but it is the truth. I swear on my mother's head. A light or something came in the room and somehow I knew exactly what I was going to do. A voice or something came into my mind:

"a comeback in hockey." I got off my knees and went downstairs and told Rose I was making a comeback in hockey. Now I hadn't played in two years and was twenty pounds overweight. It would be tough sledding.

I went down to the car company and went into the manager's office and said, "Thanks for the opportunity, but here are my car keys."

He said, "Don, I was going to talk to you. You're not cut out to be a car salesman." He was so right.

I phoned the G.M. of the Rochester American Hockey Club and said I'd like to talk to him. Now here's another strange thing. The G.M. was Doug Adam. He lived in North Carolina and only spent one day in Rochester in the summer and I happened to hit that day. He asked me to come in to see him. When I got there, he looked at this twenty-pound-overweight guy and thought it would be good publicity to give an ex-Captain a chance.

I worked my heart out to lose the weight—a rubber suit in the hot sun on a bike. Rose said, "You're going to have a heart attack."

I said, "Yeah, Rose, I could, but I'm going to make this club or die."

Training camp. I was put in the dressing room with the rookies and old equipment, me the ex-Captain of the club with rookies—another humiliating embarrassment.

I couldn't get the feel of the game back. I was doing okay but it wasn't there. Discouraged again, I was thinking of quitting, but a voice said, "Keep going."

All of a sudden it came back. I was back feeling great, playing super, getting picked as a star of the game, top of the world. But black days were coming. I was old and this was a young team. I was benched. It broke my heart. I had worked so hard. I didn't play much after that and I knew I was gone again at the end of the season. I would go to the arena and not even dress for the game. It was so discouraging. When would it end?

Before the game one night a fan attacked Doug Adam, the G.M. and coach. The team was awful and the fans took it out on Doug. To make a long story short, he made me coach. I had coached high school hockey when I was unemployed so I knew how to change lines. I was born to coach. When I was made coach, the team was eighteen points out of a playoff. We played terrific and unfortunately we missed the playoffs by a point. I was fired again by the G.M. Unemployed again.

One day Bob Clarke, the man who had me coach the high school team, called me. He said that he and eight other businessmen had bought the Rochester Americans. The Vancouver Canucks, the former owner, had lost millions. "We're taking a big chance and we want you to coach."

Of course, I said "yes" in a heartbeat.

He asked, "Don't you want to know your salary?"

I said, "I don't really care. I'm just thankful for the chance."

"It's $15,000."

"That's okay with me." I was happy even though other coaches in the league were getting $30,000.

I hung up the phone and Rose said, "Why don't you be General Manager too? You're probably the only General Manager you could get along with."

I phoned Bob back and said, "I'll be General Manager too."

Bob asked, "Same money?"

I said, "Okay, but tell me, Bob, how many players do we have?"

He said, "One."

"Who's that?"

"You."

So I borrowed and begged other teams for players. We won and packed the arena with fans. The players I had were players nobody wanted, just like me. It was us against the world. We won and just kept winning. In fact we were first overall in the league and I was rated Coach of the Year.

Bob came to me after the season and said, "The owners are mad at you."

I couldn't understand. I said, "Why?"

Bob said, "We budgeted to lose a hundred thousand dollars; but we made a hundred thousand."

Soon after I was contacted by the Boston Bruin Hockey Club of the N.H.L. and asked if I wanted to coach the Bruins. I said, "Yes."

Harry Sinden, the G.M. of the Bruins, said, "Don't you want to know the salary?"

I said, "Just give me the chance."

I remember my first game behind the Boston bench. As I looked around at the crowd and out on the ice to see Bobby Orr and all the great Bruins who I was coaching, I thought back to my room in Rochester where I couldn't get a job sweeping floors and how I asked the Lord for help and to show me the way. I remembered how black and despondent and embarrassed I was. In only three years He pointed the way and I was back on top of the world. In just three years, and they say there is no God. The Lord rescued me in my darkest hour. If you are having a hard time in life like I was and you believe, He will help you.

Sincerely,
God bless.
Don Cherry

ANSWERED PRAYER

Looking out into the universe, most of us have asked at one time or another, "Is anybody there?" Some readers may be frustrated by the silence. They may have asked that question and have yet to hear an answer. They may have asked repeatedly, persistently and received no evidence that anyone heard their cry. It has driven some to consider that there may be more to prayer than simply asking (see James 4:3–8) and others to conclude that they are not among the chosen, or that there is no God.

But others have stood under the stars and had the sense of some vast mysterious Presence that hears and knows. Encouraged by that communion of soul to soul, they may have ventured to bring a fervent longing or petition for themselves or another person to that mystery, that unknown Other, and been surprised by what could only be an answer.

How many names have been given to that One? Philosophers have tried their hand—"Unmoved Mover," "First Principle," "Ground of Being," "Life Essence," "Primal Energy." Some of the world's religions have formed around that experience and offered hundreds of names. Daringly, Jesus used a family name: "Father."

He taught His disciples to become like little children (see Matthew 18:3–4). Nowhere are we more childlike than in prayer that calls trustingly to a loving Heavenly Father. The naiveté of bringing simple, personal matters to God is a measure of a Christlike mind, for that is how He prayed. Jesus himself held a childlike faith about God answering prayer: "If you then, being evil, know how to give good gifts to your children, how much more will your Father who is in heaven give good things to those who ask Him!" (Matthew 7:11 NKJV).

There is a huge difference between luck, or what some people call "good karma," and answered prayer. Answered prayer emerges from a dialogue. It confirms a personal, caring relationship with God.

Somebody's Listening

Some divine interventions come unbidden, without any thought or prior action on our part. Such are some of the stories in this book, when out of nowhere, along came God.

But sometimes God intervenes when we ask. These responses to prayer are startling. Because they come in response to our human cry, they express a personal relationship rather than the chance operation of some mysterious force.

Karen, fifty-two years old, reported how, nearly twenty years before, her prayers of faith connected her to the God Who intervenes. On two separate occasions God showed that He was fully aware of her life situation and thoroughly involved in meeting her needs, in response to prayer.

Early in her marriage, their home had been broken into and some heirlooms taken. The emotional damage was far worse than the material loss. Her family's sense of "home" security was broken. The children became quite disturbed. Her own anxiety grew. Fearing another burglary, she began doing strange things like hiding possessions around the house. Here are her own words:

One night my husband and I went out to walk around the block. I was hardly out the door when I thought, What if we are mugged? Immediately I came back inside and took off my rings and hid them.

I then forgot about the rings until the next day when I went out in the car. Again I returned to the house, this time to retrieve the rings. I jammed them on my left hand as I walked to the car. A foolish mistake....

As I got back in the car to leave, I realized that one of my rings was missing. I had my engagement ring, the ring my husband gave me when we were expecting our second child, and my Dad's wedding band—but my wedding band was not there. I panicked!

Where was it? I searched the driveway, front walk, and steps. I went inside and looked around the front hall and the living room. Nowhere. I knelt on the carpet and cried.

At that time I was lonely in my marriage. My husband had been unemployed for a while and then was in a job I was uncomfortable with. The loss of the ring really challenged me at a deep level as to what our marriage meant to me.

I called a friend in my women's group to ask for prayer support. That evening, when I got to my class at the seminary, I asked them for prayer too. In the process, I had to confess my silly behavior, my lack of faith, my fears, and my anxieties.

The next day, as I was doing something mundane, I was diverted by a strong impulse. I sensed that I was to go to the front door, walk outside, and reach into the tall grass under the bench. It was at least five to six inches high. Following the leading of the Spirit, I did so ... and pulled out my wedding ring! I never would have found it on my own.

I can't say that we've lived "happily ever after." But I do know that God cares about me, my marriage and family, and about the trying effects of difficult circumstances in our lives.

This was the beginning of her growing faith. She has since become confirmed in her trust in God's care and protection. Her story continues:

For a few years I met with two other women for prayer, spiritual direction, and encouragement. One night as I was leaving my friend Sally's place, she told me about two fatal car accidents in her neighborhood. I laughed and suggested that it wasn't very good etiquette for a hostess to see her guests off with such stories. However, I took the time before driving home to pray specifically for the protection of God's angels and for safe arrival at my home. Then I drove off.

My route was straightforward. It was about a mile and a half down a major road from her place to mine. At that time it was a two-lane road with narrow shoulders, ditches, and farmland on either side. There were no street lights.

I was the only vehicle southbound as seven or eight northbound vehicles approached. For some unknown reason, the last vehicle suddenly came out of the line to pass. He was maybe three hundred feet away. I certainly had no time to react.

Somehow my car went on the narrow right shoulder where I traveled straight south past the now two lanes of oncoming traffic. I did not for one second swerve or lose control or even slow down—it all happened so fast. Then I was safely back in the southbound lane. I was incredibly grateful for all of our safe passings. I just praised God the rest of the way home.

There I parked in the garage, opened my front door, and collapsed across the threshold. Literally, I had to crawl into the house. I had lost all of my strength. Slowly, I crawled to the phone and called my minister. He asked specifically how I had prayed. My prayer was for protection until I entered my home. It was amazing how a head-on collision was avoided, as well as that disconcerting adrenaline surge that follows a scare. Once I was home "safe and sound," that surge literally knocked me down, I told him.

The power of those two experiences has stayed in Karen's memory as undeniable evidence of God's caring for her.

The Tie

Nothing restores the wonder of childhood more than an answered prayer. When I was a boy of eight, we had Sunday School at three o'clock on Sunday afternoon. One Sunday around two fifteen, I was in my bedroom when my mother called up the stairs, "George, it's time to get ready for Sunday School." I was busy with something and slow to respond. It was several minutes before I began to get dressed.

In those days, we wore suits and ties to Sunday School and church. As I was getting my good clothes on, my mother called again, and this time there was more urgency in her voice. "George, it's twenty-five after two. Are you getting dressed?"

"Yes, mother," I replied. But upstairs in my room I had a problem: I couldn't find my tie. I only had one tie, and I couldn't go to Sunday School without it.

I looked everywhere, in all my dresser drawers, in my closet, and on the hook on the back of my door. I even looked under the bed. No tie anywhere. Some places I even looked twice. It was now two-thirty.

My mother called a third time: "George, if you don't leave soon, you'll be late." She was angry. I knew she was right. It was at least a twenty-minute walk to the church. I had to find my tie right then.

Over my bed was a small plaster plaque with three words on it: "Prayer Changes Things." I don't know who gave it to us or who put it on the wall over my bed, but I had seen it many times. Now I got down on my knees beside the bed and prayed.

"O God, people tell me that you hear prayer. Please help me to find my tie. In Jesus' name. Amen."

I got to my feet, walked over to the dresser, and opened the top drawer. There on top of the other things was my tie. I had looked in that very drawer twice in the last ten minutes and had not seen it. In amazement I took it out and hastily put it on. Grabbing my coat, I ran out the door to Sunday School.

It made a lasting impression on this eight-year-old. Deep inside I felt so very grateful. God had heard me. He knew my need and He had answered me. God was real!

Of course, if God gave us everything we prayed for, that would be magic and we would be in control of the universe. God is God. Sometimes the time is not right. Sometimes His answer is no. Sometimes our prayers are unworthy of ourselves. By having to wait, we learn how to ask with a better attitude. We also learn that there is more to prayer than asking.

For me it opened a big window of discovery into God: Nothing was too trivial, no one too young or insignificant to have His attention.

A Remarkable Recovery

As I was nearing completion of this book, my hard drive crashed and had to be replaced. Fortunately, it was backed up to within three weeks, but recent changes and critical additions would be lost unless the files could be recovered from the old hard drive. The technician who installed the new hard drive was unable to retrieve any of the old data. The old drive would not open. On the recommendation of a friend, I called Ed Howard, a Microsoft Certified Systems Engineer, to see what could be done. When he came to my home, all his efforts were unsuccessful. Hopes of recovering the data were fading fast. As a final attempt, Ed wanted to take the old hard drive home to his lab where he would try to run a repair process. During his visit he became aware that the book was about God's interventions, and as he was leaving I said I would be praying for his success.

The next day Ed returned with the old hard drive and the triumphant report that indeed he had been able to recover the data. For an amazing fifteen-minute window the drive opened normally and yielded the desired folder. Apart from those fifteen minutes, the drive was inaccessible.

"What do you think happened?" I asked.

"Well, we did pray," he answered with a smile. For the record, I asked Ed to put the event in writing from a technical point of view. The following is his verbatim account.

"Faith in Technology"

I want to share with you a little story that happened to me recently. My wife received a phone call from a man who was referred to me through my long time accountant, now retired. You see, my wife and I run a business that supports small businesses with their Information Technology needs. Often we get called upon to assist friends and family when troubles occur with computers.

This story is about an author. He had been traveling in the United States to promote a book that was nearing completion. As I listened to the story unfold, I had a sense of deep foreboding. Stories involving laptops, travel, and large amounts of irreplaceable data such as a nascent book rarely end well. The laptop's hard drive had failed while away on the trip, and a new hard drive had been installed, and the operating system recovered. The old hard drive contained the book with the most recent changes to it, representing weeks of work. The technician had not been able to, or had not tried to recover the data. In the I.T. field this is known as "picking the low hanging fruit." Almost any technician can install a new hard drive and install a new operating system. Recovering the user's data and settings is a completely different thing.

I met George at his home office and investigated the extent of the problem with the old hard drive. I had brought a very useful tool which allowed me to connect the old laptop hard drive through a cable that I could connect to my laptop, for the purposes of data recovery. It did not look good. The old hard drive sounded poorly. (If you listen, equipment will tell you lots of things!) This one was not well. The read and write drive heads were trying multiple times to read each piece of data, sector by sector off of the hard drive. Opening the drive within Windows became a painful process of waiting enormous lengths of time while the drive tried and tried again, over and over, to read the desired data.

Reading the system's diagnostic logs, it became apparent that the drive was suffering from multiple disk input/output errors. My suggested course of action at this point was for me to bring the hard disk back to my lab, where I would run a repair process that would attempt to correct all of the sectors on the hard disk that had errors. This could mean data loss, and it may not work at all, depending upon how extensive the damage was. I was positive and upbeat with George, not wanting him to worry, but I was not convinced that the drive was recoverable.

When I brought the hard drive back to the lab, I connected it once again to the external cables that would allow me to mount the drive. As soon as I connected it, things behaved quite differently. The drive was detected by the host operating system and opened without hesitation for file access. There was no noise from the drive of read/write heads repeatedly retrying to read data—just the normal high pitched hum of a 4500 rpm laptop drive. It struck me that perhaps I had improperly attached the drive while I was at George's home office—that maybe there was nothing wrong with the drive after all! It seemed to me amazing that I could easily navigate the drive that a short time earlier I had no ability to access.

I quickly focused on retrieving the data. I navigated to the folder which George had told me contained the latest versions of his book and copied his entire profile off of the drive. Fifteen minutes later, I had a copy of his work. Breathing a sigh of relief, I now ran a disk checking utility, which took hours and hours to perform. Much later, having found numerous errors, I remounted the drive, following a clean restart. The drive was, once again, inaccessible. Disk i/o and read errors abounded— and I was never able to open or access the drive as I was able to for those brief few moments.

T. Edmund M. Howard,
Microsoft Certified Systems Engineer, Microsoft Certified Trainer
April 22, 2010

Do I Really Trust Him?

When Beatty and Barb McLean moved their young family to Florida, they had no idea how God would change them all. After a diligent search, they bought a property with a four-thousand-foot frontage on the Suwannee River about halfway between Gainesville and Tallahassee. The plan was to develop the 256-acre wilderness into recreational lots. Ironically, it had been the vision of a man who was going blind and who now became their partner. What Beatty brought to the table was unbounded energy and enthusiasm. He was a man of action. Once he made a decision, there was no stopping him. In less than two years roads had been built, causeways and culverts installed, necessary trees cut, and 156 lots surveyed, serviced, and sold. This was typical of Beatty's go-ahead attitude.

They began by making a home for themselves. There in the woods, they cleared a space and erected a three-bedroom house with a big screened verandah overlooking the river. There were other changes too. It was only a matter of months before Beatty committed his life to Christ as a result of a message he heard on the radio and not long after that before the whole family was baptized right there in the Suwannee River. But that was just the beginning.

Because the lot was on a flood plain, the house was built on cement pilings that looked like ten-foot stilts. Under the house between the stilts was some storage and parking for two vehicles. Probably while jockeying in or out of the parking space, someone had hit a pine tree which stood nearby and knocked a bit of bark off. It was a large tree almost two feet in diameter at the base and over fifty feet tall. But once the beetles and insects took over, it was only four or five months before the tree was dead. The bark was starting to fall off. Beatty knew he had to take it down or it would fall down.

That was the problem. The tree was only twenty or so feet from the house and was leaning strongly in that direction. He knew he shouldn't have left it there when he built the house; but it was in line with the center stilts so it didn't hinder parking, and it was a magnificent tree. Now, pacing around the tree and sizing it up from every angle, he realized that there was no way he could fell the tree without hitting the house. It was too big and it was leaning sharply toward the house.

For weeks he tried to come up with a solution. This take-charge kind of guy applied all his know-how and experience.

"I've got a problem. Surely I can solve it," he would say to himself in his familiar way. But short of hiring professionals who would bring in expensive equipment and charge big dollars, he could not come up with a solution. He was stymied.

Finally he told himself, "I'm stumped." He would lie awake in the night thinking about it.

Then one night he got down on his knees and prayed: "God, I'm moving this problem into Your lap. I don't know what to do with it. It's Your problem now."

The next morning he was awakened by what he knew was God's voice within him. "Get up and go and cut the tree down now," the voice said.

Now Beatty wasn't someone who heard voices. He was as practical as the next guy and more hard-headed than most. Yet these words rang with truth he couldn't avoid. It was the human part of him he was having trouble with. It just didn't seem possible or wise. But he had prayed and turned it over to God. So Beatty got up, pulled on his clothes, went downstairs, grabbed the chainsaw, gassed it up, went to the tree, and set the saw down.

"That was my first mistake," Beatty said later. "I started to think about it. I looked up that tree and walked around it. 'This is stupid,' I said. 'Every logic in me says this thing's going to hit the house and the house is going to end up in splinters in the river.'"

He was certain that God had told him to do it, but he thought he'd add a little human insurance. He got his one hundred foot rope, climbed as high as his ladder would go, and tied the rope around the tree. Then he got his wife and three kids on the other end of the rope.

"I knew in my mind that was a joke. My wife and kids couldn't make a difference to that tree. It was tons." But he still had to have some hand in it.

Then he thought, He told me to go and cut it down. I'd better get on with it. This is going to be an exciting project—either I'm going to see a miracle or I'm going to see my house collapse.

Beatty began by cutting a "V" chip out of the far side of the tree, hoping that he could shift the center of gravity somewhat. He had gone maybe twelve to fourteen inches into the tree and it hadn't moved. Barb and the kids were holding the rope taut.

Beatty shouted, "Pull! Pull!" But their heels just made tracks in the earth and sand.

Then he began cutting on the house side. He got maybe three to four inches in when the tree moved slightly and bound his saw. It was starting to go toward the house.

"Pull! Pull!" he shouted. But it had no effect. Beatty could hear some snapping and cracking as the few remaining inches of wood yielded.

The huge tree moved very slowly at first. Then, as it gained speed and began to fall, one of its top branches became caught in a crotched branch of the tall oak tree beside it, and it would not let go. Held by that branch, the pine tree was rotated a quarter turn and twisted from its original course as it fell to the ground with a resounding crash. Its trunk missed the corner of the eaves-trough on the house by less than ten inches. To everyone's relief the house was totally unscathed. Since all of the branches of the pine tree were in its top half, not even a branch of it touched the house! Beatty was amazed. It had all happened without any control or figuring by him.

This was only one of many signs which convinced Beatty not only that God was present in his life but that God could be trusted with everyday practical realities. It was just one of the influences that led him to devote twenty years to leadership in Men for Missions, a Christian outreach to various countries around the world.

The Paperclip

In the early 1980s I was applying for certification in a professional counseling organization. For weeks I had been preparing the material according to their detailed instructions. Finally, on a Friday afternoon it was complete. Now everything had to be sent to Washington, D.C. But it had taken much longer than I had anticipated and the deadline was almost upon me. To qualify for consideration that year the application and the supporting materials had to be postmarked no later than that very day.

It was four-thirty in the afternoon when I finished the application, and I was in Fergus, Ontario, Canada. I had to gather the materials together in the stamped envelope I had addressed, go to the bank and purchase a money order for US$100, put it together with the materials and application, and get it to the post office before it closed. I wasn't sure whether it closed at five o'clock or five thirty. Rushing out the door with all the papers and a large brown envelope in my hands, I jumped in my car. Wheeling out onto the street, I breathed a prayer that God would see that I got all of that done and would arrive at the post office in time.

Less than five minutes later, I parked at the curb in front of the Canada Trust office on the main street. It was 4:50 on the town clock and, looking across the corner, I could see the lights were still on in the post office. I repeated my prayer as I strode into the bank, this time with the request that I would have enough cash in my pocket to cover the cost of the money order. Prayer was my inner conversation.

There was one customer in front of me at the one teller who was open. As I waited, I put the papers in order into the envelope, being careful to keep the application on top for the bank draft to be included. It was then that I added, "And, Father, I need a paperclip."

The customer ahead of me finished. I stepped up to the counter and asked for a US$100 money order. The teller got the necessary form, filled it in, calculated the U.S. exchange rate for that day, added the service charge for the draft, and announced the total required to be $115.34. Reaching into my pants pocket, I fished out all the money I had and counted it out on the counter. It came to exactly $115.34.

Pushing the bills and coins toward her, I said, "You've taken my last cent." She replied, "That's all that I need, sir." She signed or stamped the money order and handed it to me. Thanking her, I stepped aside to put the application and money order in the envelope, and there on the counter was one paperclip.

The post office was still open when I walked in, and I asked them to postmark the envelope, just to be sure. By the grace of God it was sent off before the deadline.

At first, I was embarrassed to admit the pettiness and selfishness of my prayer and I kept this amazing story to myself. When people were starving and injustice was rampant, when millions were suffering and dying from disease and violence, I was asking God for a paperclip. This was as despicable as praying for parking spaces. I, who had decried the "success gospel" of televangelists as a denial of the cross of Christ and a gross misrepresentation of the good news of Christ's sacrifice, was virtually using God for my own convenience.

But some words of Kathryn Kuhlman, a faith-healer of that era that I heard on the radio shortly after, threw light on the issue: "The big things show God's power; the little things show God's faithfulness." Scripture also spoke to me: "Well done, good and faithful servant! You have been faithful with a few things; I will put you in charge of many things" (Matthew 25:21 NIV). I began to see that we first learn to trust God with things that are small and measurable, so that perhaps we can venture into risking the big things of our life with God as well. It is to the immature, childlike part of us that these small requests are relevant and convincing. God's faithfulness there leads us to believe He is managing the larger issues with the same caring goodness.

In that regard, the deepest lesson for me is that God's faithfulness in answering our small requests leads us to trust God's goodness in those areas where our prayers are not answered as we want. The memory of small mercies permits us to journey more confidently in those times when life becomes a desert of spiritual testing.

||||||||||||||||||||||||||||||||||||||||||||||||||||||||||||||||||||||||||||||||||||||||||||||||||||||||||

"We'll Have To Operate"

The emergency came out of nowhere. Fred and his wife Dianne were sitting in their living room with former neighbors who had returned for a visit. The neighbors' little boy was downstairs playing with their four-year-old son, Shawn, while their eight-year-old son, Don, was supervising. The calm was broken by sounds of someone gagging. Dianne flew out of the room.

No one was prepared for what came next. In a matter of moments Dianne returned with Shawn over her hip, his head pointing down, and her pounding him on the back and praying frantically. The neighbors just sat there, their eyes and mouths frozen wide in shock. Shawn struggled for breath.

"He's okay," Don announced. "He just swallowed a penny." Relief finally came as Shawn was able to swallow and breathe freely again. But the coin had passed into his stomach.

Dianne insisted that they take him to the hospital. There the x-rays revealed that it was not a penny but a quarter. Fred was surprised to discover that the stomach was located up behind the rib cage. He could see the outlines of Shawn's ribs and back bone on the x-ray and the shadow of the coin high in the stomach.

The doctor reassured them. "Don't worry. It will pass."

They x-rayed him again in a couple of days and the quarter

had just moved around in Shawn's stomach. Over the next week four more x-rays were taken. Each time they showed that the quarter was still in his stomach.

Finally, the doctors said, "We'll have to operate. It's not coming out on its own."

Fred asked about the procedure. They said they'd have to break a rib and go in and remove the coin from the stomach.

Fred thought, This poor little kid. His mind went back to when Shawn was six months old. So often it is the most troubled child who is closest to you. Fred identified so closely with Shawn because they both had similar health concerns. At six months both he and Shawn had had seizures which caused their eyes to cross and later required surgery to correct. Fred could still remember the severity of Shawn's seizure, his little fist so tightly clenched that Fred could not open it.

With the prospect of surgery Fred could only ask himself over and over, "What are they going to do with my little child?"

He and Dianne talked in more detail with the doctor. He said if the coin did not pass they would have to act by Monday, September 9—about two weeks after Shawn had swallowed the quarter.

On the Sunday before, Fred went to his minister. "You got me into this religion thing. It says 'Ask, pray, and it will be done.' If I go and have the surgery done on Shawn, it won't show much faith. If I believe that God's looking after it, why would I schedule surgery?"

He and Dianne had agreed that God can work through doctors, but he was concerned about what it would say about his faith if he agreed with the surgery. They prayed for God to deliver their son.

When Fred came downstairs that Monday, he couldn't find the Upper Room booklet that he used every day for his devotions. So he went and found an old one and just looked at the ninth day in it. The verse in that day's devotion was Matthew 15:17.

"I looked it up in my Bible and read the words of Jesus: 'Do you not understand that whatever goes into the mouth enters the stomach and passes out into the sewer?' I just cried. Tears flowed from my eyes. We first called our minister and told him. He said it was a message from God and to wait. Dianne and I agreed."

Sitting there at the kitchen table, Fred picked up the phone and called the doctor. Fumbling for words, he finally said, "I don't know how to tell you, but recently my wife and I recommitted our lives to Christ and we've been praying about this decision about the surgery. This morning I couldn't find my study book and opened another one and this is what I found."

Fred read the verse to him and the doctor said, "I understand. I'm a Christian too."

"I didn't know that," said Fred.

The doctor went on. "We'll put it off. He's scheduled to have his tonsils out at the end of the month. If it's not out by then, we'll have to reconsider."

Fred is not a guy to waffle about a decision. At 6' 2" and two hundred and ninety pounds, he's a man's man who sees faith in action terms: "If you believe, you don't keep asking. You go and do it."

He'd been communications manager for a national newspaper. He'd written his own ticket as an executive of a major Canadian corporation. He was a down-to-earth, hard-headed realist who believed in telling it like it is. But here he had been challenged to believe there could be a larger reality that would spare his tiny son the surgery. Four years earlier he had walked away from the bench of the Ottawa Rough Riders football club and onto the deserted field where they had just won the Grey Cup. He'd been invited to the big party at their hotel and was going for his car.

As he looked around the stadium he thought, There's got to be more than this! Shortly after, he and Dianne had started going to church. He was beginning to find that there was more. He believed that the most practical thing he could do was to trust the message he'd received and to wait for God to act.

One and a half weeks later, the quarter passed on its own without any damage.

For Fred, it was "a significant faith-builder." Could it have been a coincidence? "No," says Fred, "I have come to the position that there are no coincidences, just God-incidents."

A Hug To Remember

Esther lives in Michigan. On the morning of 9/11 she was packing to go to Florida when the phone rang. It was her sister calling: "Are you watching TV?"

"Why?" asked Esther.

"An airplane has hit the World Trade Center."

"You've got to be kidding," Esther replied in disbelief. She spent the rest of the morning and afternoon in tears watching TV. She watched in horror as the second plane hit the north tower. She followed the news of American Flight 77 that crashed into the Pentagon. She hung on to every report of United Flight 93 and imagined the agony of those brave souls who fought for control of the plane and finally crashed to their deaths in the field near Shanksville, Pennsylvania.

"I thought this country which I love so much would be destroyed," she said. "Any moment I was expecting something else to go on. I was in shock. What would be next?"

As it happened, on Tuesday nights she usually attended church. That night the church was full. Everyone was sobbing.

It seemed to Esther that for the next five days they nearly lived in church. She couldn't stop crying, she was so fragile and anxious. She kept praying and saying, "I need a hug and somebody to tell me everything is okay."

Esther had lived alone ever since her husband, Fred, had died in 1992. Their son had been on his own since before that. Esther had grown used to living alone. She is an independent person who enjoys making her own decisions and looking after herself. So it came as a shock to her that this national tragedy had so unnerved her. Every day she and the others around her were in tears. Every night she had trouble sleeping.

"I just kept waking up at 3:00 a.m. anxious and afraid. It was as if there was a clock in me and I couldn't get back to sleep. I couldn't find peace."

This went on for five nights. "I had cried for almost six days. I was uncontrollable and scared."

Sunday morning she woke again at 3:00 a.m. with the same feeling. As she had done all week, she prayed, "Please send someone to hold me and tell me things will be okay." She turned the light and the TV on, but the yearning to be hugged was stronger than ever. At five o'clock she turned the TV and the light off and lay back in her bed. Her eyes were still full of tears.

"Suddenly I felt an arm, a man's arm, slide slowly under my left shoulder and across my back and his strong hand grasp my right bicep in a firm hug. I bolted up in bed and said, 'Jesus is here.' But looking around, I could see the room was empty. I had no fear, only the feeling of assurance. I knew it was Jesus. I rested back into the covers and fell into a deep sleep. At 6:50 I awoke and got ready to go to church. The sobbing had stopped. The hug had comforted me. The strength I felt in that arm told me everything was okay."

Later that Sunday morning, she called her sister. "When I told her what had happened she started crying tears of gladness. She agreed with me that Jesus was here."

Processing the experience a few days later, her sister-in-law, trying to be helpful, said, "It was just Fred coming to comfort you."

"No," insisted Esther. "It was Jesus."

She was certain it wasn't her imagination, and it wasn't a dream. She had been awake. She kept thinking someone was there, even though she couldn't see anyone. "There was no human being in that bedroom, but the arm that came around my shoulders and held my arm was the most vivid experience I've ever felt."

The effect on her was profound. Not only did she stop crying, she had a peace that remains to this day. "I felt at ease over everything. Now I don't worry about anything." She has never returned to the distress she felt in those days after 9/11.

It was somewhat surprising to hear her say, eight years later, that this experience had not increased her devotion, until she explained that she had always been a strong Catholic. What that arm around her shoulder did do was prove to her that Jesus is here today in this world. "I felt this was given as a real experience in my life at a time I needed it to prove that Jesus is here with us." She knows that many people doubt His presence. Therefore, she hopes that what happened to her might help others to have faith in Him.

Running On Empty

Sometimes there is a fine line between faith and foolishness. When I recall some episodes in my faith journey, it's hard to avoid thinking of myself as either naïve or stupid. People with a practical bent might say that proper preparation could head off ninety percent of the jams we end up asking God to rescue us from. Be that as it may, the outcome in one particular case was nothing short of amazing.

It was mid-August in 1968 and I was driving home from Chicago where I had been studying. I was by myself and eager to reunite with my wife and two young children after six weeks at summer school. They were staying at her parents' home in a small town in southern Ontario. The 460 miles could be done in about nine hours, and I was making good progress on Interstate 95 through central Michigan. After the smoke and blast furnaces of Gary, Indiana, the sand dunes of the Michigan shores had given way to corn fields and orchards and the rolling countryside of central Michigan. The weather was sunny and the driving easy. It was nearly six o'clock when I stopped to buy gas on the highway an hour west of Detroit. Being on a limited budget, I wanted to take advantage of the cheaper U.S. gas prices before crossing the border into Canada. For some reason I didn't have a credit card with me. Shopping carefully along a stretch of gas bars, I found the lowest price I could and bought as much gas as my cash allowed. Then I drew the last apple out of my lunch bag and felt good as I drove on into the city.

Coming to the entrance of the tunnel that runs under the Detroit River, I realized that I had completely forgotten about the toll. Pulling over to the curb, I counted the change in my pocket; after buying the gas, all I had left was twenty cents. The toll sign said sixty cents. I backed up and parked beside a small magazine and coffee kiosk. It was deserted except for a woman who appeared to be around 40 behind the counter. I felt foolish as I explained my problem to her. Could she direct me to help?

"That might be difficult," she explained. "Since the riots, Detroit has shut down pretty tight. No one will cash a traveler's check and they're even refusing credit cards. It's Sunday night and things close up early. I don't know what you will find open."

I thanked her and drove back a few blocks. It was as she had said; the tall office buildings were like grey statues in the gathering dusk, lifeless and deserted. I found a telephone booth but had no calling card. Even if I placed a collect call, there was no way I could receive money. The more I drove around, the deeper the sinking feeling. Here in this city of millions I was stranded.

It was totally dark now. The one bright light in all my circling was that of the coffee kiosk. I returned and found the woman still there behind the counter. "No luck. Can you tell me how to reach the Travelers' Aid?" I asked.

"I'm sure they'll be closed," she replied. "But here," she said, reaching into her purse. "This ought to be enough." She handed me seventy-five cents.

I have no idea what her hourly wage was in 1968 or what that seventy-five cents meant to her in time and effort. I'm sure she wouldn't have been working there on a Sunday night if she didn't have to. The immediate effect of her gift to me, a stranger, was to transform the dark, nearly deserted city core into a friendly place. In more lasting terms it gave me one more reason to believe that helping one another can change the world. It taught me that even a small gift can have a large result. Kindness cannot be measured. What she was giving me was freedom to return home that night.

I didn't have the presence of mind to get her name or address to send her a note or return the money. I simply thanked her and went on my way.

Once on the Canadian side I breathed a sigh of relief. In three hours I would be at my in-laws' home with my family. Knowing the road and the directions gave me a sense of assurance. But an hour later I was surprised to see the gas gauge was low. I stopped to check whether there was a leak from the gas tank. Nothing appeared to be wrong. I wondered if driving around downtown Detroit had used up much fuel but concluded it would not have been much.

As I drove on, I did a mental calculation of how many gallons it would take to get home and figured it would be close. I adjusted my speed to what I had heard was best for gas mileage, and prayed. At the slower speed I became more impatient but knew there was nothing I could do about it. I prayed more frequently as the gas gauge sank toward the "E" but kept at the efficient speed. Checking the time and remaining distance, I just hoped that when the tank showed empty there would be enough gasoline in reserve.

It was now approaching midnight and if I ran out I might be spending the night in the car on a lonely country road. Again I committed my return to my in-laws' home to God in prayer.

The last ten miles I was on the edge of the seat. Any moment I expected the engine might sputter. Amazingly it didn't and at last I turned up the street in the town and brought the car to a stop in the driveway. I bowed my head and gave a silent thanks.

They had all gone to bed, after waiting up for me, and only my wife got up to greet me. I told her briefly about my delay in Detroit.

In the morning when I went out, the car would not start. The tank was bone dry.

COINCIDENCES

Once you recognize that something is a coincidence, you have been captured. A better word is "captivated," for there is a compelling fascination about an occurrence that we can't explain. Something significant has happened and we don't know how or why. Something we have nothing to do with comes out of the blue and surprises us with its timing and appropriateness.

The "what" is easy to describe. Several unrelated things happened that made sense when you looked back on them. For example, the truck that usually was kept inside on that day was parked outside just where the blast would come and it protected the people. Or, you put the wrong coat on when you went to work, but as it turned out it had the only keys in the pocket that would open the emergency supply cupboard at the office. The "how" is more difficult to explain. Coincidences have this uncanny habit of having a meaning but of happening without any evident cause—as if some script is being followed that no one in the play knows about. They give you the sense that an unseen force is working its own good design in its own way. Coincidences are God-incidents.

The Pentagon Fireman With Angels

When an American Airlines plane piloted by terrorists struck the Pentagon on 9/11, only a miracle saved Alan Wallace and two fellow firefighters. On that fateful morning, they were assigned to the Pentagon heliport fire station from the neighboring Fort Myer Army Base in Arlington, Virginia. Other Fort Myer firefighters were either at base taking a week-long course on Air Field Firefighting or were scheduled off, leaving Alan Wallace, fifty-five, Dennis Young, forty-eight, and Mark Skipper, twenty-seven, as on-duty crew that morning. Alan was in charge.

He was no stranger to danger or to miracles. Having served four and a half years' active duty in the U.S. Navy, including one year in Vietnam as a combat hospital operating room technician, and then twenty-two years as a firefighter, he had had more than his share of narrow escapes. Nothing, though, could have prepared him for what was to happen that day.

They arrived about 7:30 a.m. The fire station was new, as was the crash truck, an Emergency One Titan 3000 carrying fifteen hundred gallons of water and two hundred gallons of foam. Initially, the truck was parked in the station, a 75- by 35-foot building located about twenty feet from the west side of the Pentagon building itself. From the main doors of the station, the Pentagon was on the left, the heliport to the right with Washington Boulevard in the distance behind it. The area in front of the station between the Pentagon and the heliport was paved. Just to the right of the main doors, and around the corner, a Ford van was parked parallel to the station wall. It was used routinely to transport personnel between Fort Myer and the Pentagon.

The first helicopter flight that morning was scheduled for around 10 a.m. Top priority of the day was President George W. Bush, who was expected to land in Marine One around noon, returning from Jacksonville, Florida. Alan knew that for a Code One Standby such as that, the crowds of personnel and their vehicles could represent a risk: some might park in front of the station doors, blocking the fire truck from exiting the building. He wanted the crash truck to have easy access to the heliport in case of an emergency. So around 8:30 he pulled it out of the station and parked it on the paved pad perpendicular to the Pentagon, its back end about fifteen to twenty feet from the wall of the Pentagon, and facing west toward the heliport pad. The right side of the truck was approximately thirty feet from the fire station's main door opening.

After checking out the fire truck, eating a bowl of corn-flakes, and cleaning the station and apparatus area, Alan sat in his favorite chair in the apparatus area to read a book on opera. Mark and Dennis were inside the station in the day room. About nine o'clock Mark came out to tell Alan that an airplane had just crashed into the World Trade Center. Together they went into the day room to watch the TV coverage. It was then that they saw a second aircraft strike the second tower. After watching for another ten minutes, Alan went outside and was soon joined by Mark. They talked about the events in New York as they worked around the truck.

About 9:20, Chief Charlie Campbell called the Pentagon fire station to inform them of the attacks on the World Trade Center and to be sure they were aware that it was definitely a terrorist attack. He also said that Washington D.C. could very well be a target and, if that happened, their fire truck could be dispatched to an incident. It was then that Alan began to have second thoughts about having the crash truck parked where it was. Would it be better to return it to the fire station until around eleven or so? But he decided not to move it. And wisely so.

He and Mark had been working in the right rear compartment of the truck where the foam metering valves were located. They had just walked side by side along the right side of the truck and were about ten feet beyond its right front bumper when Alan looked up to his left. He was stunned to see a large commercial airliner crossing Washington Boulevard, about to crash into the west side of the Pentagon! It was coming in at a 45-degree angle, very low, and was only about 200 yards from where they stood.

Immediately, they heard the terrible roar of the engines. In that instant, Alan shouted "Let's go!" or words to that effect. He sprinted to his right, almost running over Mark. He had gone only a few feet when the plane hit the building. He heard the sound of it crashing into the Pentagon, sensed the waves of pressure going over him, and felt very, very hot very quickly. He ran another thirty feet until he felt certain he was going to catch fire and threw himself face first to the blacktop to get below the fireball. He found himself beside the left rear tire of the Ford van. Fearing flying debris from the impact site, he crawled quickly under the van for cover. As the heat increased, he crawled toward the front of the van.

The heat soon became unbearable and he decided to get out from under the van and farther away from the impact site. It was then that he saw Mark, to his left, standing out in the field fifty to seventy-five feet away, looking back to the impact site and swinging his arms. Alan ran to him and asked if he was okay. Mark said he was and remarked, "I'm glad you saw that plane!"

Alan replied, "Get your gear on—we have a lot of work to do. I'm going to the fire truck."

It was only then that Alan actually saw the damage to the Pentagon and the crash truck. The west side of the Pentagon was on fire from the first to the fifth floors. The plane had gone into the building at the first floor level, making a ghastly, gaping hole of billowing smoke. The floors above it were still intact and hung over the burning hole waiting to fall. The rear of the fire truck was ablaze and everything around the fire truck on the ground was on fire.

Alan raced about thirty yards back to the truck, stepping carefully through the fiery debris. He opened the right cab door and climbed in. He grabbed the radio, put the headset on, jumped over the radios, and climbed into the driver's seat. He pushed the two engine ignition buttons and, to his amazement, the engine started. He thought if he could pull the truck away from the Pentagon and swing it to the left, he could direct the roof turret nozzle into the impact site using the foam and water on board. Pushing off the emergency brake, he pulled the transmission selector into the drive range and tramped on the accelerator. But the accelerator would not make the engine run faster and the truck would not move. A lot of smoke was coming along the left side of the truck and in the open cab window. The back left side of the driver's seat was on fire, adding to the smoke in the cab. Looking to his right, he could see Dennis Young walking through the debris and was relieved that he was okay. Still in the smoky cab, Alan radioed the Fort Myer Fire Dispatch the following message: "Foam 61 to Fort Myer: we have had a commercial airliner crash into the side of the Pentagon at the Heliport, Washington Boulevard side. We are okay with minor injuries. Aircraft was a Boeing 757 or Airbus 320."

He then saw Mark signaling him to shut off the engine. Later Mark told him that whenever Alan tramped on the accelerator, the flames at the back of the truck flared up. Just as he was about to get out of the wrecked truck, someone, perhaps a Pentagon cop, appeared at the cab door asking for a breathing apparatus. Alan gave him one of the SCBA's (self-contained breathing apparatus) and handed another one to Mark. Getting out of the truck, he grabbed his helmet, radio, and face piece for the SCBA and placed them at the rear of the van where he thought they would be out of the traffic and easier to find later. All of this had only taken two to three minutes from the time of impact.

Alan assessed the situation: Dennis was attempting to put out the blaze on the truck with a fire extinguisher. Mark was removing EMS equipment from the truck. They all thought it would be consumed by the fire. The apparatus area of the fire station had been trashed and there was material burning inside it. Part of the magnolia tree which had stood near the wall of the Pentagon had been blown into the firehouse and was burning there. Alan entered through the open door and tried to get dressed in his turn-out gear. His boots and pants were covered with debris and the boots were filled with fragments of wood, rock, and metal. One of his elastic suspenders was on fire, which he stamped out.

As he was getting his boots on, he heard a man's voice outside calling, "We need help here." Alan, Mark, and Dennis, all wearing only T-shirts, trousers, and boots, went as quickly as they could and gathered on the fiery ground outside the first floor windows of the Pentagon just behind the crash truck. Alan was able to boost a civilian rescuer into the building and together with the others assisted survivors to exit through the windows. The heat was intense and the smoke and fumes made it difficult to breathe. Afterward he and Mark discovered they had second degree burns to the back of their necks and forearms from pressing against the hot window frames as they helped, lifted, and carried people from the building. He also saw that the hems of his trousers had been burned off.

When he could see no more victims to help, Alan assisted the arriving Fort Myer companies on the ground. It was then that he finally donned his fire turn-out gear. Grabbing a lantern and extinguisher, he entered the building and sprayed the areas of fire he saw. The noise of his extinguisher alerted a female victim who was then able to find her way out of the building. He also helped three men carry an unconscious man all the way out to the guard rail beside Washington Boulevard. The crash truck was still on fire, and a lot of fire was right behind it in the Pentagon. Alan began removing vital equipment, hoses, and extinguishers from the truck and then was pressed into service connecting hoses and nozzles as the Fort Myer crews were running lines into the building.

He was now feeling the effects of exhaustion and severe shortness of breath from the lack of air at the impact site. Captain Dennis Gilroy called an EMS unit who bandaged Alan's and Mark's burns and gave Alan oxygen. He, Mark, and Dennis were delivered to the triage area at approximately 11:00 a.m. where they remained for about two hours before being taken to Arlington Hospital for checking. After their release, Alan and Mark returned to the Fort Myer fire station where they found Dennis and began to tell their story and to help out. That night Alan slept at the fire station. He reflected on how very grateful he was that none of their firefighters had been killed or seriously injured.

Michael Thayer, Assistant Fire Chief, who was one of those scheduled off-duty that day, responded back into work because of the emergency and later told Alan, "Driving in, I could see the smoke twenty-five miles from the Pentagon, and I knew you three must be dead."

It was certainly realistic to think so. Investigators reconstructing the crash scene could not believe Alan and Mark had come out of it alive. Investigators wouldn't believe where he and Mark were. They measured the distance from the impact point on the west wall of the Pentagon to the front left corner of the fire truck to be 140 feet. At the moment the plane struck the Pentagon, Alan and Mark were on the far side of the truck. That would place them approximately 150 feet from the point of impact. The only thing between them and the blast was the truck, massive in itself and fully loaded with water and foam. It probably saved their lives. Looking at the truck afterward, Alan noted that something had struck the left rear wheel of the truck with such force as to bend it sideways and tear it from the axle. Similarly, considering how much damage was done to the fire station, an investigator concluded that, if the truck had not been parked where it was, the firehouse itself would have been leveled and the three people inside would have perished.

Alan has had a lot of time to reflect on the "second thoughts" he had that morning about moving the truck back into the fire station and his decision not to. He regards it as a miracle.

"The Lord has always protected me," he says, and tells how he is sometimes introduced as "This is Alan, a man who has a lot of angels."

When asked if what happened there that day strengthened his faith, Alan's instant reply is "Absolutely!"

Life Signs For A Grieving Mother

Jackie Somerville had three children, two daughters and a middle child, a remarkable son named David. Intelligent, handsome, and personable, he had a most promising future. At school he seemed to excel at everything. He was an excellent student, an outstanding athlete starring on the high school football team, and a popular student leader. In college, he was in the business program, was president of the Student Council, and was valedictorian in his graduating class. Jackie fairly glowed when she told others how gifted he was in playing the guitar, singing, and acting in school productions. Then at twenty-five, in a tragic

early-morning boating accident, his life was snuffed out. The un-
thinkable had happened. He, who had been her joy, was dead,
gone. Her heart was ashes. How could she ever live without him?

In the numbness of her grief she went back over his life
endlessly with her husband and daughters, recalling this detail,
that family time together, and poring over pictures of him, as if
remembering him could bring him back. At his graduation he
had performed the song by Garth Brooks that he loved so much,
"The River." Jackie played the tape over and over and could hear
him singing it again:

> You know a dream is like a river
> Ever changing as it flows
> And a dreamer's just a vessel
> That must follow where it goes
> Trying to learn from what's behind you
> And never knowing what's in store
> Makes each day a constant battle
> Just to stay between the shores.
>
> And I will sail my vessel
> 'Til the river runs dry
> Like a bird upon the wind,
> These waters are my sky;
> I'll never reach my destination,
> If I never try.
> So I will sail my vessel
> 'Til the river runs dry.

Too many times we stand aside
And let the waters slip away
'Til what we put off 'til tomorrow
Has now become today.
So don't you sit upon the shoreline
And say you're satisfied.
Choose to chance the rapids
And dare to dance the tide.

And I will sail my vessel
'Til the river runs dry
Like a bird upon the wind,
These waters are my sky;
I'll never reach my destination,
If I never try.
So I will sail my vessel
'Til the river runs dry.

There's bound to be rough waters
And I know I'll take some falls,
But with the good Lord as my captain,
I can make it through them all.

Yes and I will sail my vessel
'Til the river runs dry
Like a bird upon the wind,
These waters are my sky;
I'll never reach my destination,

If I never try.
So I will sail my vessel
'Til the river runs dry.

Yes, I will sail my vessel
'Til the river runs dry.
'Til the river runs dry.

It was uncanny how well the words fit David's life, almost as if he knew what was coming. She found it comforting to think that and to sense the strength of his faith and character through the song. But her grief needed so much more.

Jackie threw herself into therapy. She did heroic grief work, tending his grave religiously, honoring his memory, working through her loss, and expressing her feelings of anger, sadness, and regret until she was drained almost beyond endurance.

With her husband, Bruce, she also sought help from a grieving parents organization. To some extent the solidarity with others who were going through similar trials gave her strength. Yet hearing their tragic stories overwhelmed her. She had more than enough difficulty coping with her own loss without taking on theirs.

Initially, their extended family and friends rallied around the grieving family, as did their wide social and professional networks. The time came, however, when some acquaintances and more distant friends began to show signs of battle fatigue. After what seemed to them a realistic length of time, they subtly expected Jackie and her husband to be getting over their loss.

But they could not. It was hard for some to understand what they were feeling. Nothing could ever replace him. Life would never be worthwhile again. She and Bruce began to withdraw from trusted long-time associations. In all of this the best help came from a quite unexpected quarter. They, and particularly she, began to have spiritual experiences that convinced her of David's survival in a world beyond this.

For the most part these took the form of repeated "appearances" or "signs" that pointed to him. Soon after his death she began to see subtle evidence of his presence in her world: When she went out into the garage to do some painting, she noticed the letters "I C U" painted on the wall. She thought it strange and asked her husband. Bruce explained that a few weeks before his death David had painted those letters when he was testing a can of spray paint. It might not have mattered except for what followed. Their youngest daughter owned a dance studio and was in the throes of deciding whether to re-locate to a larger facility. A prospective new landlord had offered her space in his building and she asked her parents to come with her to inspect the premises. Still deep in grief, neither of them was in any frame of mind to offer business advice. Yet Jackie was her assistant at the studio and decisions of this magnitude were usually treated as a family matter. So Jackie and Bruce agreed to at least have a look at the new space. "As we were pulling out of the parking lot," Jackie says, "the prospective landlord drove out ahead of us. To our surprise, his license plate bore the letters 'ICU.' Even my daughter, who is a skeptic, agreed that this was a sign to move forward."

Hardly three months after the tragedy, her older daughter had a remarkable experience at the same college David had attended. On her first night of teaching classes, it helped soften the sharpness of the moment that the location where she was teaching was some distance from the campus where he had studied. She arrived early and was looking for a place to sit down in a crowded hall where hundreds of people were milling around. At last she spotted an empty place on a bench and claimed it. As she sat down, there on the seat beside her was a picture of David staring up at her from a school newspaper. Underneath the picture was a poem written and dedicated to him by a student advisor. Remarkably, that was September 12 but the date of the newspaper with the picture and poem was September 2, two issues earlier. Even stranger, that single page with his picture on it was the only part of that newspaper there on the bench beside her. Until that moment no one in the family knew anything about that poem or the picture. Reflecting on this amazing occurrence, Jackie says, "How often our hearts had cried out, 'We know where your body is, David, but where is your wonderful spirit?'" This was one of the early signs that he was alive somewhere and was communicating with them.

Another sign came several months later. Because her concentration had been so frazzled by the tragedy, Jackie had been reluctant to drive long distances on her own. When she finally attempted it on country roads and was driving home alone for the first time, she found herself in a snowstorm. The poor visibility unnerved her until a red Mazda truck pulled in front of her and led the way through the storm. It looked exactly like David's red

Mazda truck he had loved so much. To her surprise and great comfort, it led her all the way to her hometown with its familiar streets and lighted roads. For Jackie that began a repeated occurrence. "From that time on, whenever I was driving long distances by myself or in unfamiliar places, a red Mazda truck usually found its way to lead me to my destination."

Fully a year after his death, two more signs were given that spoke to them of David. The first one occurred when Jackie was driving home from their family cottage early in the morning on her way to work. She was by herself when a red Mazda truck passed in front of her. The image of a license plate flashed in her mind and she thought, Wouldn't it be something if I saw a license with his nickname on it? Hardly two minutes later a car drove in front of her with a license bearing his nickname, "OX." The name came from his football playing days.

The other sign came several months later when she and Bruce were driving home from the cottage, their hearts still heavy with remembrances of him. Overhead was a stunning blue sky, totally clear except for a billowy white cloud formation in the shape of a butterfly. Incredibly, on the tip of the butterfly wing was a rainbow. "It was most unusual," Jackie says. "I have never seen a rainbow where there had been no sign of rain." It was another touch of hope for them.

As is usual in cases of tragic grief, birthdays, anniversaries, and festivals bring back memories that are now very painful. For many years all three of her children had worked at an apple orchard and Christmas tree farm owned by very dear friends of Jackie and Bruce. David was especially close to Sandra and Blaine, the owners' children, for whom he would baby-sit. When he had worked at the apple orchard in the fall, David would drive the tractor taking people out to pick apples in the "pick your own" operation. At Christmastime he also drove the tractor to take people to find their trees and would dress up as Santa for the kids. He had a hearty "Ho! Ho! Ho!" that he loved to sing out.

The first Christmas after David died, Sandra arrived at Jackie's house in tears. She had come directly from the mall where she had purchased a Christmas ornament for them. It was the annual ornament put out by Hallmark, a one-of-a-kind creation each year. In that year, 1994, it was Santa on a tractor, waving. Sandra couldn't believe her eyes. She bought one for each member of Jackie's family and her own. The ornament touched Jackie deeply: "You don't very often think of Santa on a tractor, and why was it in that particular year? I have looked every year at Christmastime since and have yet to see anything similar to this particular ornament."

On the first anniversary of David's death, they buried his ashes at the nearby cemetery. Jackie remembers it as a brutally miserable day. "Friends came for a short service and we stood in the pouring rain under umbrellas throughout the readings and ceremony. Just as David's ashes were lowered into the grave, the sun burst through the storm clouds and stayed maybe five minutes. Then the rain poured down again. All who were there were transfixed. It was like a message saying, 'I'm okay where I am. That's not me that you're burying.' It was very emotional."

These "sightings" extended over a period of three years. She found great comfort in them. They reassured her of his well-being and love for her. She took them as evidence that he was alive, albeit in a different dimension, and knew what she was doing.

One of the most significant coincidences occurred on her younger daughter's wedding day, more than two years after his death. It was a day that understandably reinforced the fact of David's absence. As her husband and their daughter were being driven to the church for the wedding, a car pulled in front of the limousine they were riding in. Its license bore the word "KID"—the very nickname he had called her because she was the youngest. The car drove ahead of them for several blocks.

What gave these coincidences such power was that they were so personal. They expressed David's individuality and uniqueness. They embodied favorite hobbies, activities, and mannerisms and were extraordinary in expressing things that only the immediate family would know. They "fit."

For Jackie these signs had a deeply spiritual power, even a religious meaning, which she badly needed. Although she and Bruce were practicing Christians, she struggled with uncertainty about a heavenly Father. God seemed remote to her. Perhaps because she never had her own father after age three, she had trouble seeing God as part of the process. When tragedy struck, the Christian teaching of resurrection and heaven seemed detached and irrelevant to her. As she said, "I needed the here and now." That was exactly what these sights and signs gave her: the strong sense that the universe was dependable. Her son was not just out of touch, lost in the remote place she thought of as heaven. He was communicating here and now. So in a very real sense these signs strengthened her faith in the unseen world of God and brought a measure of peace to her aching heart.

Where Acorns Land

The phone rang in Steve Richardson's★ high school guidance office. The mother of a seventeen-year-old girl was calling to ask for help.

"No one has been able to get through to my daughter," she lamented. "I have tried professional counseling agencies, alternative education, grounding, bribes, everything, but she just won't go to school and if she does, she's late and doesn't try."

Her story went from bad to worse. "Her father is a schizophrenic on a disability pension and has been very severely depressed for the last two years. One of my other children also refuses to go to school. He is very low functioning. The work is just too hard for him."

As if that wasn't enough, the distraught woman continued, "And I am on a disability pension for my back injuries. I don't know what to do. Can you help?"

There are days in a guidance office when the problems seem almost overwhelming. This school is in a distressed part of a major city with more than its share of heartbreaking situations—drugs, violence, racial strife, family breakup. This woman's story was unfortunately becoming common.

"Can you bring her into my office?" Steve asked. "I'd like to talk with both of you." As a Christian, Steve believed in miracles. As he hung up the phone, he knew he would need one.

The next day an exhausted looking mom and a lifeless, withdrawn daughter sat in front of him. He listened again as the woman recounted her tragic story. He helped her identify those particular factors that might have brought her daughter's education to a standstill. Sarah* agreed with her mom on the history, her behavior, and her resistance. She admitted she had no interest in school, was not attending, and had hardly attended the year before. Sarah had no idea why she felt this way. Before that, she had been a good student, earning mostly A's and B's.

Steve considered what could possibly break the chronic cycle of depression that gripped her. They talked about having a purpose in life. That soon bogged down in the face of Sarah's hopelessness. How could he help her claim a positive attitude? Steve turned to a media resource he had developed for teens to show the wonder of the human brain. He flicked on the slide presentation designed to illustrate the amazing efficiency of our learning processes. It showed how powerful the brain is, able to process some 400 billion bits of information per second. "Of these," it said, "we are only aware of about 2000. That means our brains process 200 million bits of information for every one we are aware of." The presentation went on to make the point that each of us has huge learning potential. All that is required is being willing to apply the brain we have. Sarah watched but said nothing. Turning it off, Steve talked about how hard it is to change our behavior, but how rewarding. Sarah politely listened and answered his questions. But she was unmoved. She had simply come to please her mother and had no intention of returning to school.

Not ready to give up, Steve remembered a series of slides he had just prepared. He decided to see how she would respond to them. They told the story of an acorn who didn't want to change.

Sarah smiled when she saw the acorn art. Steve had drawn eyes, a nose, and a mouth on a picture of an acorn. He explained "'Austin the Acorn' really likes himself the way he is and sees no need to change. Austin is perfectly content to hang out with his friends where it is warm and sunny." Steve showed a slide of many acorns.

He continued the commentary: "Austin thinks the other acorns who get all dirty and mucky in the ground are dumb."

The next slide showed an acorn in the ground growing a leaf. "This acorn has a vision of himself as a tree. He chooses to attract the resources he needs, like moisture, warmth, nutrients. Every day this acorn with a vision grows and attracts more nutrients and moisture. Austin laughs at this acorn with the puny little leaf and makes fun of him." Sarah smiled.

The next slide showed further growth. "As it draws more nourishment and moisture to itself, roots, leaves, and branches grow from inside that tiny acorn. Finally, it becomes a strong, tall oak tree." He showed the final slide of a mature oak tree.

Then Steve finished by asking Sarah, "If this little acorn can grow itself into a big oak tree, isn't it possible that you might be able to attract the resources you need to reach your vision in life? Since you have that amazing brain that processes at 400 billion bits of information per second, all you lack is a clear vision of the person you want to become."

Sarah smiled for the third time. "I like that story," she said. "'Guess I'm being like Austin." At last there was the flicker of a connection.

Steve seized the moment to stress the importance of affirmations, of making positive statements about herself and her abilities. He gave her examples of how these could help her mentally see success before she actually achieved it. Sarah seemed a little bit interested.

Near the end of their meeting word slipped out that Sarah was hoping to go with her schoolmates on a three-day school trip. Her mother said firmly that she wouldn't be going—money was tight. Thinking quickly, Steve offered to find funds to subsidize her field trip if Sarah would attend every day for the next six weeks until Christmas break. Sarah seemed unconvinced but agreed.

There was the slightest hint of hope in the air as Sarah and her mother stood up to leave. All the while Sarah had been wearing her gray winter coat. Now she zipped it up and thrust her hands into her pockets. Then a strange look came over her face. Her eyes went wide with surprise as she slowly pulled her left hand out of the pocket. In it she held an acorn.

"I don't know where that came from," she exclaimed.

Neither did Steve. Mother and daughter left without further comment.

Steve's hopes that the deal they had made would work out were soon dashed. Three days later she stayed home, proving the promise of travel funds was no incentive. He continued to work with her, however. The school allowed her to drop a course, leaving her with three subjects and the requirement to check in with Steve during her now free period. He used these brief meetings to encourage her. With his prompting, she made a list of affirmations and repeated them to him in these sessions. He gently promoted the vision of a life of purpose. After several weeks she was definitely making a better effort to attend but still had some stay-at-home days. From her point of view the only difference was that now she felt guilty if she stayed home.

One day Sarah's mom wrote a note to excuse Sarah from being late because they had both been up most of the night at the hospital. Her father had attempted suicide. Steve was impressed that, when she could have used this family crisis to stay home and count on his sympathy, instead she came to school late with the note.

The last day of school before Christmas, Sarah sought Steve out after the school assembly. She thanked him for believing in her when she didn't. She asked him why he had been so kind to her and had spent so much time and energy on her.

Steve explained it was because he believed she could do it and in fact she had improved, even if it was not up to the level they both had hoped for. This was the reason he was a teacher—to help kids like her. He told her how proud he was of her for getting caught up in her classes and for coming back after being away for so long. He revealed that he frequently told his wife how well Sarah was doing.

The words sparked something in her. Steve no longer saw a broken-spirited child before him. Sarah's face showed the growing strength of a woman of purpose. She stepped forward and gave him a huge hug. Ever so slightly she had started on a new path.

As she walked away Steve reflected on how she had changed over the past two months and what might have contributed to it. He recalled how from time to time she would mention the acorn story and how finding the acorn blew her away. He wondered what she had done with that tiny symbol packed with potential. Had she held it in her hand, imagining the future wonders it contained? Had she put it under her pillow and slept on it, or kept it in her pocket to remind her of her possibilities? He didn't know. But something told him that from that very small beginning a sense of purpose had begun to grow.

The Pool Cue And The Open Door

It was 1970 Montreal, a time when clergy were still a vital strand in the social fabric of Quebec. The telephone rang in the home of the Reverend Gordon Allan, minister of Madison Baptist Church. A young man of eighteen had been charged with battering of a child less than two years old and they wanted someone who spoke French to be in court with him. Gordon was not fluent in French and so he arranged for a French-speaking pastor and friend of his to be there. Gordon went along to listen.

The young man, Raymond,★ and his wife or girlfriend, Monique,★ sat together in the courtroom. The child was her daughter. It was not clear whether Raymond was the father. Raymond was already deep in other troubles and over the next thirty years he would spend as much time in prison as out.

The judge impressed Gordon as a thoughtful and caring man committed to rehabilitation rather than punishment. As the proceedings unfolded, he noted Gordon's presence in the court and viewed his involvement in a favorable light. When Raymond was given a brief sentence to Bordeaux jail, the judge asked Gordon privately if he would be willing to accept responsibility for Raymond at the end of his sentence if he were released into Gordon's custody. Gordon replied that in his judgment it would be unwise because then he would be identified in Raymond's mind as part of the system. A compromise was struck in which Gordon agreed to maintain unofficial contact with Raymond and offer a supportive friendship when he was released.

Meanwhile, Monique had been sent to jail on a related charge. Gordon remembers her as an emotionally unstable young woman who was chronically unable to stay out of trouble. He went to visit her in jail. In the course of ministering to her he happened to read a passage to her which mentioned incest.[4] He has no idea why he read that particular passage, but she was quick to reply: "That's what my stepfather did to me when I was twelve." The pieces began to fall into place and Gordon began to see how damaged she was. Issues of trust and intimacy with men were crucial for her.

A few moments later she asked him, "Have you visited Raymond?"

Gordon replied, "I've never met him." Technically, he had only seen Raymond at a distance in court.

The next time he visited Monique she told him that Raymond would like him to visit him. Gordon saw this as an early opportunity to form a bond with Raymond and he went twice while Raymond was still in Bordeaux jail.

---

4 1 Corinthians 5:1.

When Monique was released, Gordon was named as her parole officer. Soon after, when Raymond was released, Gordon began the unofficial mentoring relationship with him agreed upon with the judge. For the first two months Monique kept her appointments with Gordon and things were looking hopeful. Then, without warning, she disappeared. During those two months Gordon had nurtured a growing relationship with Raymond as well. But now he had disappeared too. All of Gordon's efforts to find them failed. He was no stranger to the fickleness of human nature or the frailty of human resolve. It was the end of the line, or so it seemed. He knew his limits and surrendered them to God in prayer.

One morning a few weeks later Gordon had a lull in his schedule. He had received a letter from a church in Brockville, Ontario. They had a ministerial vacancy and were inquiring whether he might be interested. Sitting in his office in Montreal at 10:30 that morning, the thought came "out of the blue" to get in his car and drive the 125 miles to Brockville, just to get the feel of the community. Who knows where these impulses come from? How can anyone explain why we take action on some and not on others? Usually he had a crowded schedule, but that day, for some reason, it was open. Getting in his car, he drove the two hours to Brockville. There was no appointment, no one to see. He just had a hamburger on the outskirts of town and drove aimlessly to the downtown area to look around.

He remembered a restaurant by the riverfront where he had met with friends years before and went looking for it, without success. Leaving the river, he drove north the two short blocks to King Street, the old highway to Montreal. For some reason, instead of turning right in the direction of Montreal, he turned left. He had gone only a hundred feet when he heard a man calling from behind him, "Reverend Allan. Reverend Allan." It was Raymond.

Gordon pulled over and they chatted briefly. Monique was at a restaurant down the street. Raymond had been shooting pool in a pool hall. It was a warm day in May and the door was open. As Raymond was lining up a shot, he looked along his cue and beyond, through the open door, saw Gordon driving by in his car at that very moment. Dropping the cue, he had rushed out and chased after him.

Raymond went back and gave up his game. Gordon circled the block and picked them both up. They reconnected over coffee and brought Gordon up to date. Raymond was out on bail. Monique was in one of her restless flights. They explained they were not running away from him and were glad to see him.

In as gentle a way as possible, Gordon said, "Didn't you know I was concerned about you? I had no way to contact you." They made apologies and tried to explain.

At one point Gordon said, "I had to trust that God would direct you to me. Is there any other way I could have found you?" The point was not lost on Raymond.

All three of them knew that the chance of their meeting as they did was beyond all probability. It was certainly opportune for Monique because it meant that Gordon had seen her now for three straight months, which fulfilled her parole requirement. For Raymond it went deeper. It became the basis of a warm and trusting relationship between the two men.

Over the next thirty-four years, he and Gordon would be in touch on a regular basis. Sometimes it would be visits to Raymond in jail, sometimes Raymond visiting Gordon at his church or home. Sometimes Gordon would receive a card or letter or phone call from Raymond telling him about his life. He knew Gordon cared deeply about him. They would often talk about God and pray together. Gordon used many of those opportunities to tell his young friend about God's love for him in sending Jesus to die for his sins and of the help available to us through the Holy Spirit today. Raymond made more than one commitment of his life to Christ with Gordon. But Gordon was never sure how deep Raymond's professed faith actually went because he kept messing up his life and having to pay for it. Under the influence of questionable friends and unwholesome environments, he would fall easily to temptation. Against that background, the relationship he had with Gordon stood out as a positive. It was a constant Raymond could count on.

This is by no means a success story. Soon after that reunion in Brockville Monique and Raymond broke up. Rumor had it that she had picked up with a wrestler. Gordon has not heard from her since. Nonetheless, the story of Raymond's long acquaintance with Gordon is positive in several ways. A relationship of honesty, trust, and caring such as theirs is never fruitless or wasted. Who can tell what depths Raymond might have gone to without the lifeline to his friend Gordon? If the remarkable encounter that day in Brockville has been an indelible memory and inspiration for Gordon, what must it mean as Raymond reflects on his own life and worth? As Gordon said to him that day of the pool cue incident, "You'll never have to wonder again whether God knows you or cares for you."

DREAMS

Most people who remember their dreams take no credit for creating the dreams they have. There are some few people who believe they are able to "incubate" dreams by focusing their mental images prior to sleep, but the vast majority of dreamers experience their dreams as the creation of another mind—their unconscious or God. Contributing to that belief is the originality of most dreams. They often contain a wisdom and even foresight that go far beyond the ability of the dreamer. Also, many dreams surprise the dreamer with their aptness to their actual life situation. All of these factors add to the sense that dreams put us in touch with an ultimate or divine mystery.

From Cynic To Bluebird

If you've ever crouched over an old-fashioned outboard motor trying to start it on a damp morning, you know it often takes a series of pulls before it catches. The same goes for a gasoline lawnmower. At first, pulling the crank cord may bring only one or two firings that sputter out. It's only when you get that third and fourth "catch" that you know it's going to go.

In baseball it's the same story. Apart from a home run, winning is usually a matter of putting singles, doubles, triples, and walks together in a series that cumulatively scores runs. It's the accumulation of many individual plays that finally wins.

Sport imitates life. In life it often takes a series of positive factors, or you might say coincidences, to bring a desired outcome. As if you had to thread not one, not two, but three needles before you were in a position to successfully thread the fourth.

Betty Marsh is a case in point. For almost twenty years, she had been driving the same sixty miles on weekends from her home in the city to her recreational farm and back without stopping once in Fergus to buy anything. But then she listed the farm for sale and on that one occasion went into town to visit the realtor's office. Next door to the office was a convenience store where she stopped and bought a copy of the local newspaper. It was a weekly paper with very limited circulation and she had never read it before. In it she happened to see an ad for a dream seminar to begin the following week in a neighboring town. There was something about it that attracted her. Even though it was on a weeknight and would require her driving one hundred miles round trip from her home for six weeks she registered for it. She had recently retired and could consider such an arrangement. So it happened that Betty was one of six attendees at the first dream seminar I offered in the fall of 1981.

It was a critical time in her life. For several years she had been director of an education college course specializing in the training of primary-level schoolteachers. As a single woman, she was devoted to early childhood education and derived great satisfaction from fulfilling that role. It was her passion. Then, through a change in political policy, the school had been closed. At fifty-five years of age, she had been forced into retirement. Now, two years after the school's closing, she was still trying to adjust to the loss. The dream she shared in our first session states better than any words how she felt about her life. It simply showed four white porcelain dinner plates, arranged in a square formation, one cracked, all of them empty.

As part of the introductory process that first night, I mentioned in passing that the subject of my PhD dissertation had been on spontaneous regressions of cancer. The next morning my telephone rang. It was Betty.

"I now know why I saw your ad and why I had to come to your seminar," she said. "This morning my doctor phoned with word that the biopsy of my breast lump was malignant. Will you take me as a client?"

Life suddenly became intensely busy for Betty. Tests and medical consultations became almost a daily occurrence. On top of that she and I began an intensive program of supportive psychotherapy almost immediately. It included visualization and relaxation, lifestyle counseling, dream work, and prayer. She was an eager and well-motivated client who was thoroughly involved in her therapy. In addition, she enrolled in a program of nutritional counseling.

The first major challenge came early: the cancer treatment team to which she was referred strongly recommended surgery to remove her breast along with adjacent lymph nodes. She hesitated for several reasons, including the fact that there was no evidence that the nodes were diseased. No alternative was offered and she felt trapped.

"I don't want to be disfigured," was her firm response.

Her surgeon then referred her to a different cancer facility for an independent assessment. All the while Betty and I continued with two or three sessions of psychotherapy weekly. It was a full six weeks after the initial biopsy when the second facility reported their findings and recommendations. The essence of their report was "we find no malignancy, only scar tissue from the initial biopsy." They recommended a course of twenty-one radiation treatments as a precaution. Betty was understandably relieved.

Two nights later she had the following dream: "I am the only person in a theater where a dress rehearsal is being held. Dominating the stage is a large wooden cross with a noose hanging from it and a trap door underneath. 'Surely they're not going to show that [execution],' I said to myself. The only person on the stage was a fat man who was making his way off stage. His coat collar is pulled up hiding his face, but I can hear him chortling with delight."

In discussing the dream, she was certain it referred to her probable death. When I reflected with her on the two forms of execution, crucifixion and hanging, I recalled that earlier she had spoken of treatment by radiation and surgery as a kind of "double death." Then I asked her about the man on stage who was obviously delighted with the coming death. She understood that figures in dreams could represent parts of the dreamer's self. Could there be a part of her like that man?

"Yes," she replied. "He's my cynic."

Up to that very moment, Betty had vigorously maintained that she wanted to live and believed that she could survive the cancer. She had been exuberant about the benign test results. The dream of the cynic, coming two days later, suggested that an unconscious part of her doubted the test results and further that, at some level, she may not want to get well again. That awareness of a negative attitude, which could be classed as an unconscious death wish, gave us a focus for our work over the next several months. It permitted us to engage consciously in the conflict between her negative and positive attitudes toward life.

Visualization can be a powerful way of focusing one's mental and spiritual energy for healing. Among various visualization techniques, I suggested that she make a collage to represent her life at that time. What she produced was a stark black and white page with a few pictures of objects cut out from magazines. There was a noticeable absence of any natural or human figures.

Throughout January and February we continued to address the depressive elements that were emerging, using standard techniques now interwoven with collages. Gradually color crept into the scenes, natural images, flowers, trees, and animals, and some individual human figures. By mid-February one of the collages included a pair of eyeglasses, possibly the symbol of a new perspective coming into focus. Her emotional tone was more upbeat and her energy level vibrant. By March the collages featured human figures interacting, usually in reciprocal and cooperative roles. Her dreams kept pace, picking up more hopeful images and capping this more positive dynamic with the dream of a wedding in which attendants arrive on horseback. By Easter the cynic seemed to be vanquished when her collage was crowned by a full-color picture of a bluebird.

Confirmation of her renewed sense of worth was not long in coming. Almost immediately she was invited to give a summer school university course in her beloved specialty. It went a long way toward cementing her newfound confidence and sense of purpose.

For the next four and a half years Betty was cancer-free. Then she returned to tell me that a lump had been found in the same breast where the original biopsy had been taken. She said she had decided to have the lumpectomy her doctor recommended. The operation was completed successfully and she remained cancer-free for the next twenty-four years.

Sometimes life can be like a stream that hardly flows but lingers in lazy ponds and deep pools. For long stretches it scarcely seems to move and one could be forgiven for thinking it was going nowhere. Then it comes to a narrow place where there are rocks, and it rushes through twists and turns, swift and furious. With each bend a new vista unfolds as the water is driven to some unforeseen goal.

With her forced retirement and the initial cancer diagnosis, Betty had come to one of those narrow places. But it was a breakout for her. Looking back now, she sees it as a time to learn who she was, a time to know there is power available to get better and to get the help she needed. Most important, she learned what needed to be changed for her to find meaning and fulfillment in retirement. As she says, "I gained confidence that life wasn't over." What followed was typical of how she participated in her own healing. She embarked on a program of wellness education, took retraining courses, and served her church for over thirteen years in volunteer work that she found both interesting and satisfying.

There were many helpers other than myself on her healing journey. With God life can be such a wonder of fortuitous connections. Her healing was a team effort involving medical, surgical, and non-medical personnel, the strong support of caring friends and family, and the support of a church prayer group to which she belonged. Any of these helpers might have their own knowledge of how circumstances lined up to bless her in her treatment and recovery. From my perspective I see clear evidence of a guiding hand at work beyond what she or anyone else could do for her—for example, in providing the second cancer treatment approach and its benign biopsy report, or in giving her the cynic dream. Or, to return to the threading-the-needles metaphor and our therapy together, she had driven the same road for years, but just when she needed it, she bought a newspaper, saw the ad, registered for the course, and did the work. Indeed, several "needles" had been threaded and a series of beneficial "coincidences" drew her forward on a course she had not foreseen or wanted but that was designed to bring her to a healing and far more abundant place in her life.

Only now, in the fall of 2010, after twenty-four years in the clear, Betty has been diagnosed with cancer again. Again she has come to a narrow place in the stream.

The Medical Alert

One of the most powerful ways in which God speaks to us is through dreams. They can sound a warning or alert us to a danger that requires our attention. Consider the case of Susan, a forty-eight-year-old woman who was in good health and would never have guessed that anything was wrong.

At first she thought it was a mosquito bite, just a small irritation on the back of her right thigh. It was summertime and she was wearing Bermuda shorts that brushed against it. But weeks later it was still sensitive whenever her fingertips would touch it. Further examination revealed a slight rash around it, and she made a mental note to book an appointment with her physician, which she forgot to do. Another week passed and then she had the following dream:

"I am standing in the corridor of a very busy place. Everyone who passes is wearing white lab coats so I realize I'm in a hospital or intern's residence. I'm very concerned about a rash on my leg and feel certain someone here can help me. Everyone is moving with such purpose that I'm not sure who to approach. I interrupt a female doctor who's passing. She declines my request, saying gynecology is her field. I plead that a quick look may be enough to determine if it needs further attention. She agrees to check if we do it right here and now. I stretch back my leg to straighten it, exposing the rash on the back right thigh. I turn my head back to explain things to her and see that she is already crouching down and examining it. One or two others have joined her to give their opinion as well. To my surprise, the rash has spread and covers a much larger area. I feel comforted watching them, knowing that they know much more than me."

When she awoke, she realized that she needed to check out the tiny growth on the back of her leg. She promptly called the doctor's office and was seen later that week.

As she waited in one of the examining rooms, she noticed her surroundings were all related to gynecology. Posters on the wall showed diagrams of the female anatomy and the stages of pregnancy. Pamphlets addressed issues of female sexuality. She chuckled, thinking of the dream.

Eventually the doctor appeared—a female doctor. She was substituting that day while her regular male doctor was attending a conference. The doctor examined the rash, studying it silently for a full minute. She then left the room and returned shortly with a second doctor. He was the woman's regular physician, who had come back early from the conference. Together they crouched down to examine the tiny abnormality, using a large magnifying glass.

Susan was standing. As she turned her head to the right and looked down to talk with them, she was astounded to view the two crouching doctors examining her leg in what was an exact frozen "frame" from her dream. The doctors agreed that the lesion was highly suspicious and needed immediate attention. A few days later it was successfully removed in the hospital and proved to be cancerous.

The woman was immensely relieved to have the threat removed. Equally, she was amazed by the prompting that had come through her dream. What kind of wisdom had known the seriousness of the growth five days before the doctors examined it? Who or what had foreseen the precise pattern of that specific scene when the doctors would kneel beside her and make their diagnosis? And what had the power to produce that knowledge into a dream that warned her and that she would remember? In her mind there was no doubt: the dream was a gift of God.

HEALINGS

We've become accustomed to taking a physical view of health, even though we know the mind and spirit are intimately connected with the body. In the last twenty-five years, it has been shown clearly that negative emotions are destructive to health, while positive emotions like hope and faith and love have a healing effect.[5] So the way is open to see medical and spiritual factors as partners in healing.

In this, as in so many things, we are rediscovering ancient truth. Believers in God have always known that the power that made the body can heal the body and that faith is a powerful ally in healing. Much of Jesus' ministry was in healing—of body, mind, and spirit. The stories that follow show that cooperation.

"That Artery Isn't Supposed To Be There"

Dave was in need of a healing miracle. Though he didn't know it at the time, he was about to have a heart attack. All he knew was that something was not right. At forty-nine, as a high-functioning person loaded with responsibility, he just kept pushing himself.

5. Bruce H. Lipton, PhD, *The Biology of Belief* (Carlsbad, California: Hay House, 2005); Dr. Paul Martin, *The Healing Mind* (New York: St. Martin's Press, 1997); Norman Cousins, *Head First: The Biology of Hope* (New York: E.P. Dutton, 1989).

At the school where Dave taught, space was severely limited. When mold was discovered in his portable classroom, plans were made to replace it. However, a new portable would not be available for three months. Dave was offered the choice of remaining in the portable for that semester or teaching his classes on the stage in the school auditorium. He chose to remain in the old portable, mold or no mold. But those three months wore on him.

As Christmas and the end of term drew near, the stress grew higher. Dave developed a strep throat infection and went on medication. Finally, at the end of the term, he had just finished moving all the classroom materials to be ready for the new portable when a severe pain gripped his left arm. He lay down for half an hour. When the pain did not abate, he went to the hospital.

There his blood enzymes showed a mild heart attack had occurred. They kept him in the hospital for three days then sent him home. The pain continued, however. He had no energy. It was an effort just to walk down the street. He was given a stress test. The cardiologist reported there was a blockage of some sort and gave him some nitroglycerine to relieve the pain. He was also given a beta blocker and advised to change his diet and undertake an exercise program.

Dave was determined to do everything necessary to restore his health. He took a leave of absence from the school, bought a treadmill, read every book he could find on heart disease and heart healthy diets, and applied everything he had read and been advised to do. He changed his diet, drank more water, exercised faithfully, avoided second-hand smoke, and got lots of rest. After four months being off work and on this healthy regime, he went for a nuclear stress test. It was inconclusive. He was still having chest pain and was very tired.

When he had done all that he could and had been off work for five months without any improvement, the discouragement began to take hold of him. "It doesn't seem to be getting any better," he told himself. "I'm so tired I don't think I'll ever be able to go back to work." He was now so worn down that he began praying with resignation, "Lord, if you want me to stay this way, I'll accept that, or if you want to heal me. Either way is all right. I'm reconciled with either outcome. You know best. You just do it."

As a boy, Dave had "known" some unseen power guided his life. But not all the time, by any means. He had lonely days and times when things went wrong, just like other folks. But when it mattered he knew someone was looking out for him.

That had become clearer and clearer as he grew up. When he was sixteen, he was spared almost certain death in a swimming pool accident. Another boy was first to dive deep and was electrocuted by a cracked underwater light fixture. Dave, who loved swim class and was always first off the board, had not been feeling well that day. In fact, he had asked to be excused from the class and was sitting it out in the gallery when the accident happened. Because he had special training, they called Dave to give mouth-to-mouth resuscitation. As he worked over the student, he thought, This would have been me. After that he never forgot how he had been spared.

Dave had been raised in the church by loving Christian parents. Baptized at twelve, he was active in the worship and youth programs of the church. But in his late teen years he lost all interest in going. All he saw was hypocrisy and meaningless ritual. By the time he went to a university at nineteen, he was very negative about religion, and his early faith had vanished. Even then, as Dave says, "God found me." During orientation week, someone from Campus Crusade asked for volunteers to take a survey on religion. Dave was more than willing to tell them his bitter criticisms. The last question, though, was the one that got him. "Would you be interested in knowing God personally?" His heart spoke, "Yes, I would." For some time he had been feeling that all his best efforts to live fully on his own terms had failed.

It took a month of wrestling with God's Spirit and talking with the man who gave him the survey until Dave handed over control of his life to Christ. He had a great sense of peace. In the months of spiritual growth that followed, Dave came to understand the further need to be filled with the Holy Spirit. When he finally made that his prayer, God filled him. "I was really changed. There was this incredible joy and love." It was then Dave clearly saw that God's purpose for him was to be a teacher. So even though he was now facing no improvement in his health and he was disheartened, Dave was not without hope that God would bring him through somehow.

As a final follow-up, Dave was scheduled for an angiogram. In that procedure a catheter is inserted through an artery and a dye is released that highlights on a monitor the blood flow in the arteries of the heart, revealing any blockages. The night before the angiogram, Dave still had the same symptoms of pain and lack of energy. In the middle of the night his wife was awakened with a sense of purpose. "I really can't describe it," she says. "You just know some things. I just knew I should lay my hand on Dave and pray for him. I did that and asked the Lord to open up his arteries and to make them clear."

Dave slept right through it and was unaware of what she had done. She then fell back into a peaceful sleep. She had to work early the next day and so a friend drove Dave to the hospital.

There in the heart imaging suite they prepared him for the procedure. The doctor and technician took their places and began. On the monitor screen overhead, Dave could see the catheter enter the heart area. He was surprised he had no sensation of it and felt relaxed, almost detached, as if he were watching a TV program.

He paid little attention to the routine instructions and comments as the doctor released the dye from the catheter within the heart. There was silence as the team watched the irregular lines of the coronary arteries being traced out and highlighted by the dye. Then the doctor's tone changed. "That's unusual," he said, half to himself. "He's got an extra artery here." On the monitor overhead he pointed out to Dave the two main arteries that supply blood to the heart muscle. With his finger he traced the clear image of a third artery growing between them. "That artery isn't supposed to be there." The doctor said he had never seen anything like it before and afterward gave Dave a picture of it to take home.

No blockages were found; in fact, they saw no need for medication or treatment of any kind. Dave was given a clean bill of health.

Dave felt the change. He felt normal again. "I knew I had the energy I had before." His wife picked him up at the hospital, and on the drive home he told her about the extra artery. It was then she told him how she had prayed in the night. They just looked at each other.

The next day Dave felt good enough to go out and play nine holes of golf. It was at least two years since he had felt able for that. "I never thought I'd be playing golf again." Now he breezed around the course.

The real test came in walking up the steep hill to the ninth tee. "There's no way I could have walked up that hill before that miraculous change." Yet that day he walked straight up and without any hesitation or shortness of breath.

Considering what Dave had been through during his five-month absence from school, the principal urged him to take the summer off and return in September. It was the end of May, and Dave might have done that without any qualms. But he felt so good and had so much energy that he went back to school two weeks after the angiogram, just in time to plow into one of the heaviest periods in the school year—the year-end reports and finishing procedures. This man was healed. As he says, "God did His own bypass surgery."

What has happened in the ten years since? "My heart has been great. I have lots of energy; don't need medication. I just watch my diet." At fifty-eight, Dave feels like a young man again

A Date With Healing

Some years ago I was deeply impressed by the unusual healing that occurred for a woman in her mid-sixties. I had known her and her husband for twenty years as a minister and then as a friend of the family.

A fluke following a successful bladder operation had led to a fistula of the bowel. The surgical incision had not closed over and was complicated by the ulceration of the bowel beneath that lay open to the air and would not heal. Her condition was chronic. She had lain in the hospital for over three months, going from bad to worse. She could pass no solid food, and daily she grew weaker on intravenous feeding. A growing sense of hopelessness settled in.

At the nursing station I asked about her progress. The nurse replied with unusual seriousness, "We're worried that she's so depressed."

A quiet visit followed, supportive and safe. At first, we talked around the subject. But both of us knew the gravity of her situation. Finally, the moment could be put off no longer. But whether to risk the miracle question...? I ventured, "What would you want most, if you could have it?"

She closed her eyes and thought long into the silence. Then she said in a steady voice, "To be home with [my husband] and able to live a normal life together in retirement."

I almost gulped out loud. Do I dare believe it is possible? Am I raising false hopes? Under these circumstances is it realistic? Ethical? But her life was in the balance.

"Let's ask," I urged, bolder now and with a brashness that surprised me. "When would you want to be well enough to go home to him?"

"By Thanksgiving," came the rather quick reply. The Canadian Thanksgiving was less than two weeks away. I thought, I'm not quite that confident, and suggested giving it a little more time. We looked at a calendar and settled on a date two weeks after Thanksgiving.

"By the 26th, then," she said finally.

So we prayed, boldly asking for definite healing by that definite date. Before leaving, I wrote "26" on a slip of paper and pinned it in the middle of the cards on the notice board opposite the foot of her bed where she would see it often.

There followed one of those remarkable times when everything seemed to be moving in slow motion to what we already "knew" would be happening. A vital energy seemed to gather within her. The open wound began to heal from the inside and gradually to close over. Color began to return to her face. Slowly she could tolerate food. The intravenous came out. She grew stronger day by day. You could see the hope in her eyes.

Two days before the 26th she went home. In a matter of weeks she made a complete recovery and lived fifteen more years together with her husband before he died. Then four months later, with a loyalty she had kept throughout their long marriage, she died peacefully.

Misdiagnosis?

The initial response to a miraculous healing or extraordinary occurrence is often skeptical. People often pass it off as "only one of those mysterious coincidences." We become accustomed to diagnoses of terminal illnesses leading in weeks or months to the death of a relative or friend. That is usual and expected. But some people with serious or "incurable" illnesses experience an unusual time when the illness reverses and they make a total recovery. Some would call that a miraculous healing; others regard it as just a coincidence.

That was the debate in the case of Frank★, a fifty-three-year-old Mennonite pastor-teacher whom I interviewed in a study of spontaneous regressions of cancer. As he sat smiling with his wife in their sunny living room, he told me of the chill that had come over his life some thirteen years earlier when abdominal symptoms drove him to seek medical help. Persistent pain and two series of x-rays taken weeks apart confirmed the presence of a walnut-sized growth in his lower bowel. In short order surgery was scheduled to explore and remove what had the markings of bowel cancer.

Initially, his response to the possible diagnosis was shock and fear. Cancer was a dreaded word to him. He recalls the realization, "I have cancer. Cancer equals dying. I'm too young to die."

But it was not his nature to let his feelings out, so he did not let anyone know that he expected to die. In his typical upbeat way he responded by making his relationships more intense and tried to make the best of everything. He told others, "I'm going to live as long as I can for the glory of God."

Gradually his reaction became a kind of resignation: "If this is God's will, I can handle it." He remembers telling himself, "I've always loved the Lord. If it's time to go home, it's time to go home." He continued his heavy work schedule with a "business as usual" attitude right up to the time he went into the hospital. Privately he had a kind of quiescence: "I just waited for a time when I could be operated on, with no real burst of faith or expectation of anything; just, I was being prayed for. I have cancer. Cancer means death. Okay. Whatever the Lord has is okay."

In contrast, he had Pentecostal friends who believed in miracles and who said quite directly to him, "God's going to heal you. You may not even need to go through the operation. We're just going to start praying."

Part of him rebelled against the glibness of this; yet it comforted him to know that they and many others were praying for him daily.

A severe bout of pain led to his being admitted to the hospital five days before the scheduled operation. Those five days presented Frank with a unique experience. He saw himself not as a patient but as a chaplain to those around him in the hospital—something he had not been able to do before in his remote rural ministry.

"I wandered around in my robe," he said, "talked with people, and was able to pray with some of them. There was a piano in a room where the wheelchair patients would come and we would sit around and sing. Doctors would go by and say, 'Oh, do you know this song?' and so we'd sing it. That place was like a little chapel. People were encouraged and one young man gave his heart to the Lord…."

His five days of ministering to all sorts of people in need gave him a peak experience of elation about what his ministry could be. Frank spoke of them as "days of encounter." The open wards were his parish and there was enthusiastic response to his ministry. Hearing him tell of those days on the wards, there is no suggestion whatever that this man was facing death or was depressed about the inadequacy of his work, or even that he had the least fear of what lay ahead.

The operation went ahead as scheduled. When Frank regained consciousness, he heard his doctor's surprising report: "We found nothing wrong; but you're going to have double the ordinary discomfort for a while. I went over your intestines inch by inch to be absolutely sure!" Frank, who was a devout Christian and had many people praying for him, believed he had been divinely healed just prior to the surgery. He was discharged and ten days later had a final examination. The surgeon was pleased with Frank's recovery and shared his belief in God's healing.

Was it a divine healing or was it the healing effect of those five days of bliss he experienced as chaplain on the wards, in his "days of encounter"? Or was there some other explanation?

Later, when I attempted to verify the medical data of the cases for my study, I contacted the surgeon, who was by then retired. I explained my need to qualify the research I was doing and asked about Frank's case. Although it had been thirteen years previous, he remembered the case quite clearly.

To satisfy my request, he reviewed Frank's file. He reported that although the symptoms, x-rays, and tests strongly suggested the presence of a walnut-sized growth in the colon, the actual surgery revealed no growth whatsoever. He concluded that there had never been any cancer. He thought that a tendency to spastic bowel might explain the x-ray image and pain. In his judgment it had been a misdiagnosis.

Yet the symptoms never returned, and thirteen years later the man was a picture of good health. Misdiagnosis or divine healing?

"I Want To See"

The following story was written by the late Reverend Linda Riesberry, a registered nurse and chaplain in palliative and pastoral care. She died on February 8, 2007. Linda shared a forty-year ministry with her husband, the Reverend Canon Bill Riesberry, an Anglican priest, in Toronto and Orangeville, Ontario. The following story comes from the early 1990s when she was still a lay person. The Linns to whom she refers were Matt Linn, a Jesuit priest, his brother, Dennis, a former priest, and Sheila, Dennis's wife. They have an international ministry based in the United States.

"OPEN OUR EYES, LORD"
Blind from birth, Mary★ simply requested, "I want to see!"

We had spent the day hearing the Linn Brothers teach us about healing. Now it was time to put the teaching into practice. Those who needed prayer for healing were instructed to rise from their theater-like seats and stand, signifying their need.

The rest of the people were asked to gather around anyone nearby, ask what the prayer need was, and then lay their hands on the person and pray silently for five minutes for that person. "Be Jesus to the person," was the instruction. What that meant I had no idea. In fact in some way I thought it was a bit presumptuous. Three of us lined ourselves up around Mary, a tall 40ish woman near us, one on each side of her in her row and me reaching out over the seats in front of her.

On one side of her a short elderly priest said, somewhat patronizingly, "Well, dearie, what can we do for you?"

Her reply was quiet and simple: "I want to see."

The priest was quite taken aback and the woman on the other side almost faded out of the picture.

My scientific medical nurse's mind inwardly said, "Impossible." Then I asked, "Do you just need to see better without glasses?"

"No," she said. "I have been blind since birth."

Then breaking through the sense of overwhelming helplessness came the leader's instructions again, "Get on with your praying and just be Jesus to whoever needs His healing." In obedience we began.

In silence. Five minutes at first seems like a long time! It was in that time that I heard God tell me how to pray. It was also in that time that I struggled and reasoned with God about why I couldn't or shouldn't do what I heard Him saying. Very clearly I heard Him say, "Lay your hands upon her eyes."

"I can't, Lord! You know as an Anglican I'm not to do the Laying on of Hands and especially on the head."

"Lay your hands on her eyes," came the persistent charge over and over again.

After what seemed like an eternity (in actual fact only a couple of minutes), I gave in and laid my right hand across her eyes. That moment for me was a profound experience of God—a real theophany!

Then breaking through the awe came some more instructions from the front of the room: "Check with the person with whom you are praying and see where she or he is at."

We all opened our eyes and to our amazement Mary read my first name, which was in larger print on my name tag. She said, "I can only read your first name. Your last name reminds me of the story of how the blind man Jesus was in the process of healing saw trees walking!" (see Mark 8:24). We were awestruck to put it mildly!

Mary continued speaking directly to me, "You know when you put your hand on my eyes, it was not your hands I saw, but I saw the hands of Jesus. I saw Him as soon as you touched me."

At this point further instructions were given: "If the healing isn't complete, pray more. Continue to pray in Jesus' name." Another five minutes.

We went back to silent prayer. With expectation this time. No hesitation about laying hands on her eyes. At the end of the five minutes Mary opened her eyes and read what she said was a clear first name and a slightly blurred last name. God had not only opened her eyes but had also taught her to read. Awesome!

People were encouraged if they needed continued healing to go home to their prayer groups and have loving, soaking prayer until the healing is complete.

God works through our simple prayers, our listening to Him, and our obedience in acting on His Word to us. "Glory to God whose power working in us can do infinitely more than we can ask or imagine!" (Ephesians 3:20).[6]

Hopeless, But Not Impossible

After a cancer self-help workshop I conducted in the mid-1980s, one of the participants sent me a newspaper article she had cut out years before. I think it was from the late 1970s. It was written by a retired medical doctor in Newfoundland and I believe it was from a Newfoundland or Montreal newspaper.[7]

In the article, the doctor told of a woman who had been admitted to a hospital there with an advanced case of tuberculosis of the lungs. Because she lived in a remote outport, her condition

6. From a post-communion prayer in *The Book of Alternative Services of the Anglican Church of Canada* (Toronto: Anglican Book Centre, 1985) 214.

7. If anyone has information about this article or this woman's healing, please contact me. I've been unable to find the clipping in my files and have reconstructed this story from memory and brief summary notes I made at the time. Every effort to track the article down has been fruitless.

had gone undetected and was now critical. The lower portion of her lungs had been consumed by the disease. The only possible hope in such cases would be radical surgery to save the remaining healthy parts of her lungs; but the cavity created by the disease was so great that they could not be certain of enough healthy membrane to fashion a secure enough diaphragm for the healing of her lungs to take place. Without the pressure normally created by a healthy diaphragm, each breath would threaten to burst the newly constructed lung sac. Reluctantly, they had to abandon any hope of saving her life and be content to maintain her in as comfortable and humane a manner as possible for as long as she survived.

They settled into a program of providing the best medical care and social support they could under the circumstances. Without knowing the grim prognosis, she persevered bravely and was a cooperative patient. However, she missed her husband and family greatly and, as Christmas approached, asked if she might go home to have Christmas with them.

The treatment team met to consider her request. They weighed the obvious benefits of a loving family, familiar surroundings, and the joy of the season against the tiring trip, the lack of emergency medical treatment, and the drain on her dwindling physical resources.

Given that she was going to die soon anyway and that this would likely be her last Christmas, they concluded that it would be an act of compassion to grant her request and that it could do her more good than harm. They consented and sent her home for Christmas, half expecting that she might die at home.

When she returned in January, they sensed something different about her. She was slightly more upbeat and cheerful. They concluded that the risk had been worth it and that the family time had strengthened her. They were not prepared, however, for the discovery several weeks later that she was pregnant.

The treatment team quickly assembled to assess this dire new development. A therapeutic abortion seemed mandatory. How could she possibly bring this pregnancy to term, much less deliver it successfully? To bear the child might kill her even sooner than the tuberculosis. And, if by some fluke, she did manage to have the baby, how could she hope to care for it with her grave medical prognosis? But the ethical consideration weighed heavily. She dearly wanted this child. She was opposed to abortion on principle. Also, they feared the negative effects of her losing the pregnancy which had created a new energy in her. Feeling that they were walking a tightrope, they decided to let the pregnancy continue and to monitor her situation even more closely. After all, as long as it went forward it was doing no harm.

Without burdening her with their added concerns, the medical team supported her pregnancy as normally as they could and were surprised at how well she coped. Not only did she maintain the pregnancy, but she grew stronger as it progressed. Contrary to their worst fears, at full term she delivered a healthy baby girl.

That in itself was a major achievement considering her near-death condition at the beginning. But the pregnancy had produced an additional benefit. In the latter months of her pregnancy, as the baby grew within her, it pushed her diaphragm upward to fill the cavity in her lower lungs which had been ravaged by the disease. It achieved exactly the healing maneuver that the surgeons had seen originally as the only hope of saving her life. Her recovery was remarkable and within weeks she was pronounced clear of disease and able to return home with her baby, who was thriving.

The medical doctor, who had retired by the time he wrote the article, concluded by saying that those events had happened years before. He had it on good authority that the baby daughter, then in her early twenties at the time of his writing, and her parents were busy preparing for her wedding. The mother had never relapsed and was enjoying good health.

LIFE-CHANGING ENCOUNTERS

Science helps us understand how natural changes take place. Often we can see the actual processes working and measure the results. When human nature is changed, however, we are in the area of the Spirit of God. I am speaking now of moral transformation, of character being reshaped to different values and attitudes and of people's relationships being rewritten in a new language of understanding, patience, and love. Lives become infused with a new energy and purpose.

We grope to understand the mechanism at work, for these things are hidden. Somehow an outer circumstance and an inner situation fit together at the right time.

A person comes under conviction, is repentant about past sins, believes a word of Scripture is for her or him personally, or is open and hungry for the Holy Spirit. Through a series of events or the influence of another person, life takes an unexpected new direction. In each of the following stories, whether it was a driven man finally coming to the end of himself, a desperate woman being visited by the living Christ at a crucial moment, a techie sitting in a bar receiving a revelation through an image that came to his mind, a youth coming under the influence of inspired preaching, or a hardened ex-con finding love in the form of a chicken farmer, the persons involved met with God and were changed.

Extreme Measures

Jim* pointed the sawed-off shotgun straight at the teller's face. "Gimme your cash. All of it. And keep quiet."

The terrified woman did as she was told. Jim scooped the bills into a bag and ran out of the bank. Jumping into his car, he sped off.

This was the stupidest thing he'd ever done. It was his hometown, in broad daylight, and everyone knew him. His father was pastor of one of the larger churches in town and what he had done was contrary to everything he'd been taught.

But then, Jim had done a lot of stupid things in his young life—like getting drunk, doing drugs, recklessly racing fast cars. Once, he and his friend souped up a 400 hp Mustang to over 500 hp and raced it on the back roads up to 200 mph. Power was thrilling to him. If he could get it to 150 mph, then he wanted to go 170. And if 170, then 180. When he never got caught for speeding, it just made him want to go faster. But each broken limit bored him and he yearned for more. He measured a man by how daring he was. Soon he was pushing all the limits a young man of his day could try.

All the while he had kept his place—attending church, singing in the choir, going to the youth group. He played the church game of pretend on Sunday, while living on the wild side the rest of the week. Amazingly, he never got caught. No one found him out, even in that small town where everyone knew everyone else. They all kept their church face on and accepted his.

In time, his younger sister and much younger brother had taken their places in the church and had become respected members of the community. Unlike Jim, they both lived straight and decent lives without feeling they had to break the rules to prove themselves. His kid brother had later joined the police force in a large city nearby. In his own pursuit of risk-taking, this brother volunteered for the elite scuba-diving unit of the force. He excelled in the rigorous training and reveled in dangerous assignments. Each day he would put his life on the line to save others.

Jim, however, found that every limit he broke without getting caught just made him bolder. It was intoxicating. With the bank robbery, however, he finally met something too big for him to push. The world was now against him. He had become a criminal, a wanted man. He fled across the border to the States. There he drifted from town to town, always a fugitive, constantly looking over his shoulder. Every police unit had his description, and he knew the noose could close on him at any moment.

What had once been so thrilling had lost all its excitement. Life itself had become empty and meaningless. He missed his home, his family, his friends, his freedom. In his loneliness, he began to slip morally and, worse still, not to care. Somewhere in his misery, his thoughts went back to the story of the Prodigal Son (see Luke 15:11–24) he had heard about in his church days—how the boy had impatiently asked for and received his inheritance ahead of time and had wasted all of it in sinful living. Jim knew that he, like that boy, had come to the place of desperation where pig food would be better than what he had.

He was like an animal without a soul. He had hit bottom and was in a deep depression. Thoughts of suicide became stronger and more frequent.

He was in Jacksonville, Florida, when he made the decision. How does one prepare for such a step? Slowly, he climbed a radio tower, intending to jump to his death on the cement culvert below. It was then, near the top as he looked down, that something remarkable caught his attention. A car was making its way slowly near the base of the tower. It was a white Buick—the same year, the same model, and the same color as his father's car—identical down to the pattern of rust marks on the same wheel well. It turned his mind to home again. He thought of his father, who he knew loved him. He would be devastated by his suicide. The spell was broken. Then and there, Jim decided to return home to his father in Canada and face the consequences for his crime.

The judge sentenced him to six years, and he was sent to a maximum security correctional institution. Though he had been slightly humbled, there was still a lot of the wild man in Jim and a lot of self-will and stubbornness to be dealt with. Over the course of his time, he received a total of one hundred and eighty-eight stitches to his head, the price of daring to be himself in prison.

But he was not forgotten. His girlfriend, later to be his wife, wrote to him daily. Every other Sunday, as soon as church was over, his father and mother would gather her and their care packages into the family car and drive the three hours to the prison. They would visit him for one hour then drive the three hours back. Their love and faithful support made a deep impression on him. After twenty-two months, he was released and returned home to the same small town and to his father's church.

No one can predict what form the agents of change will take or when they will come in one's life. Whether they will ever come cannot be presumed. If and when they do come, it is a miracle. For all the trouble Jim had gone through, including his near suicide and his time in prison, he was still rebellious, unrepentant, and pushing the limits with drugs and drinking. It would take a real miracle to change this man.

God's agent on special assignment in Jim's life turned out to be a Mennonite farmer who befriended him on Jim's return from prison. This man believed in him, prayed for him, and would not let go. For a time it was a fierce battle.

The farmer was a hulk of a man weighing over 300 pounds—someone Jim could not ignore and had to respect. Although he had a gentle spirit, as many large men do, on occasion the farmer would physically confront Jim to make a point. One time in church he planted himself solidly in the side aisle, blocking Jim's way. He was working on Jim's need to control and push everything. Jim's anger grew so hot he was ready to hit him, but he thought better of it. Such was the intensity of the struggle between them. After many months of this, the moment came. Kneeling on the farmer's living room floor, Jim finally surrendered control of his life and accepted Christ as his Lord and Savior.

This was the turning point in Jim's life. The change took. He married his long-time girlfriend and they began to raise a family. He went on to be a successful businessman, the head of a respected company, and a community leader. Today he and his wife are happily married, with two grown children and four grandchildren. Amazingly, this former convict is bonded for over $1,000,000—a further sign of how gracious God has been to him.

There is a footnote to Jim's story. A few years after his conversion, the enormity of what he had done began working on him. The custom had developed for him and his wife to visit his in-laws in the same small town where he had grown up and to have Sunday evening dinner at their home. Nearby was the home of the woman who had been the teller in the bank the day of the robbery. Jim had held the shotgun in her face when he robbed the bank. Now he realized the terror he had brought into her life. If he had pulled the trigger that day, it would have been this woman he would have shot and almost certainly have killed. He felt strongly that Jesus was telling him to go and ask for her forgiveness.

After supper one Sunday, Jim went and knocked on her door, but there was no answer. He went back the next Sunday with the same result. For nearly a year, each time he would go over to apologize, he would find no one home. Finally, when he knocked, the woman's husband answered. Could he speak with the man's wife? Yes. The wife was called and Jim went into the living room. Once they were seated, Jim told them that the Lord had given him a ministry to do but that he could not do it without asking her forgiveness first. With his voice quavering, he blurted out his apology and begged for her forgiveness. What he did not know was that she had attended a conference where he had given his testimony some months before and knew he was a changed man.

She also knew that coming to her and her husband like that to ask for forgiveness would be one of the hardest things for Jim to do. Yes, she would forgive him. If God could forgive him, she thought, I can forgive him too. And she did. There were tears and they prayed together. Then he got up and left.

He heard nothing more until much later. Ten years went by when he gathered with other men from churches across Ontario, Michigan, and Ohio to go on a work bee to build a church in Sierra Leone. There in the group was the woman's husband carrying a toolbox. He was one of those in the building crew. They would be boarding the same plane and working together. Throughout the long flight Jim felt uneasy about the man's presence in the group.

After they had been at work a couple of weeks on the project, as part of a devotional time of sharing, the leader invited them to apply the scriptural teaching by affirming one another. Each of the sixteen men would draw the name of one other man in the circle and say something he admired about that person. Jim began to pray furiously within himself that this man would not draw his name. But that is exactly what happened. Jim expected the worst.

When it came his turn, the man stood up before the group and said, "I've known Jim for many years. We grew up and lived in the same small town. Back then Jim did something that hurt my wife quite badly. Let's say he wasn't exactly my wife's best friend. One Sunday, years later, we were surprised when Jim appeared at our door asking to speak with my wife. He told us that Jesus had sent him to ask for her forgiveness. Then he sat down with the two of us. He apologized in tears and begged her to forgive him. Jim does not know this, but when he had left, my wife and I were stunned. If Jesus could direct Jim to come like that and ask her forgiveness, then maybe we should consider doing the same ourselves with the people we hurt in our daily lives. My wife especially was blown away by it. This man who had hurt her so badly was now her friend. And that's what's been so good working here alongside Jim. There's been such a marvelous change in him."

Jim was the most surprised person in the room. He could only marvel at how much had changed since that day when he held a shotgun in that same woman's face. God's grace knows no limit.

High Over Michigan Avenue

Marci* was a twenty-eight-year-old flight attendant based in Chicago. She was divorced and living with three other flight attendants on the nineteenth floor of a high-rise overlooking Lake Michigan.

One night she was alone in the apartment and desperate. Standing by the window high above Michigan Avenue, she thought, There's no screen on this window. I could just sit on the edge and fall off.

A young woman her age had gone off the roof just a few months earlier. It had been working on her mind. The thought terrified her. What if I did do it? My family would soon get over it—I'm not very close to them.

Marci's family life had been pretty chaotic. There was a lot of fighting and unhappiness in the home. When she was five they had moved from Toronto to Detroit. Overwhelmed and isolated, her mom had a complete nervous breakdown and was hospitalized for a long time. Her parents had divorced when Marci was in high school, and she had gone off to college.

Standing there by the window, Marci thought, I've got to call somebody, but who can I call? I can't think of anyone who would really care if I lived or died.

Growing up she'd been a loner, with few friends. After college she'd had the magical idea that in the airlines she'd meet a man who would make her life complete at last. The first part worked out well when she was hired by a major airline. But the pilot she met was an alcoholic who was abusive when he drank. She found that out when she married him, but with her low self-esteem she thought, Who else would marry me?

It lasted a year and a half, and she could take no more. She was depressed, crying all the time, lonely, and scared. She had to get out for her safety and her sanity. She left her marriage.

After the divorce, Marci found herself thinking that the problem was the man she'd married. She decided she'd go back into the airlines and get the right man this time. Amazingly, the airline re-hired her and she did meet another man. But this relationship was even worse than the first. In a matter of months she was more miserable than ever. She became involved in things with him that caused her not to want to live anymore. That's what brought her to the edge of oblivion that night high over Michigan Avenue. Just sliding off the sill would end it all.

In that moment, she remembered something she had seen on TV a few nights before. While flipping through channels looking for the Tonight Show she had stumbled on the 700 Club instead. A man was talking about the problems we have in life and how at the bottom of them all is human sin. We have all rebelled against God, he was saying, and cut ourselves off from God and the life He wants for us. But God did not leave us in our mess. Because God loves us, He provided a way back for us by sending His own Son to live a sinless life on this earth and to die on the cross instead of us. She listened as he continued telling how Christ rose from the dead, overcoming sin and death for all of us, and how anyone believing in Him is promised forgiveness and eternal life.

At the time Marci had thought, Well, that's probably true. But I don't know … these people are so religious. They pray; they read the Bible all the time. I don't know anything about the Bible. I can handle life. And she had turned the TV off.

Now, as she stood alone at the window, she realized she really couldn't handle life. She felt she was going to die. In that moment of terror, she cried out, "Jesus, if You're real, help me. Help me!"

She couldn't see Him, but she felt absolutely certain that Jesus was there in the room with her. Later she recalled, "I felt enclosed in His love and I felt Him saying to me, 'Marci, I love you. Don't do that.'"

For the first time in her life she realized she was an unclean person in the presence of holiness. She was a sinner. She started to think of all the things she had done and said in the past. "Oh, how I wanted to go back and change them. But I couldn't; they were past."

Then she heard as clearly as any human voice, "I forgive you."

This brought her to tears.

"Every time I thought of some sin, in my mind I'd say, 'Oh, not that'; He would say quietly, 'I forgive you.' I'd think of another thing, and He'd say, 'I forgive you.' And on it went, every time I'd think of something I'd done He'd say, 'I forgive you.' I felt like a terrific weight was lifted off of me and I knew everything was going to be all right. It was an incredible night."

But there was more. A few days later, as she was preparing for work, something kept repeating itself over and over in her head that she couldn't stop. Then she recalled that someone had told her, "If you can't forget something, write it down on a piece of paper. Then it'll be on the paper and you will forget about it."

In the airport limo, the same thought came into her mind again. She got a piece of paper and wrote it down. But what she wrote made no sense. So she just folded the paper and tucked it in her wallet.

A few hours later, in the Cleveland airport, she was buying something when she found the piece of paper in her wallet and looked at it. A light went on. She wondered if what she'd written was in the Bible. She finally found one at a bookstore there at the airport. Until then, Marci's knowledge of the Bible had been nearly zero. She had tried to read the Bible in motel rooms, but she couldn't make sense of it. It seemed such an old book with strange names and places.

What Marci had written on the paper looked like "I Z E A 12 1." Flipping through the pages, at last she found something at the top of a page that sounded like "IZEA": Isaiah. It was a whole book in the Bible. She went to the twelfth chapter, verses 1 and 2, and read, "In that day you will say: 'I will praise you, Lord. Although you were angry with me, your anger has turned away and you have comforted me. Surely God is my salvation; I will trust and not be afraid. The Lord, the Lord himself, is my strength and my defense; he has become my salvation'" (NIV).

Marci realized this wasn't just any old book. As she says, "The living God was speaking to me! He was saying, 'You know what happened the other night was real and I am real. I was angry at your sin. But I've forgiven you and am not angry anymore.' I could hardly wait to get home and buy a Bible and start reading it."

That was 1975 and Marci has had many years to reflect on her life before and since those moments by the window: "Looking back I realized that all my life I had been looking for happiness. I had thought happiness came from marriage. Now I realized that it wasn't happiness I really wanted, but peace. I never, ever had peace until I found the Lord Jesus. One of the first verses I memorized was John 14:27: 'Peace I leave with you; my peace I give you. I do not give to you as the world gives. Do not let your hearts be troubled and do not be afraid'" (NIV).

Today, this beautiful woman says with a full smile on her face, "You see, I have really come to know that Jesus loves me, that God is real, and that He loves you too."

She is alive because of her amazing encounter with Jesus.

Detours And Destiny

When an established pattern or direction in one's life is dramatically altered, it raises questions about the power and purpose of the disruption. If a log floating in the current of a great river, for example, is suddenly diverted from the straight course it was on, one would look for the possibility of a strong side current from an incoming tributary or the influence of a submerged rock or obstruction. So when a trend-line that has become set and predictable takes a new direction, we may assume that some new power has entered the picture.

My teenage years in Ottawa had taken on an almost boring regularity. After three years at the same high school, living in the same house on Aylmer Avenue in the Ottawa South district and chumming with the same friends, things had settled into a familiar groove. I knew my way around town, had learned where all the major stores and places of interest to me were, and traveled a great distance each week by public transit for my violin lesson. I would spend Saturday afternoons playing either football or hockey with the guys, doing odd jobs around the house, or watching the double feature at the local movie theater. On Sundays I'd occasionally go to the Anglican Church where my dad sang in the choir, or sleep in, or play chess with my intellectual friend, King.

Then life changed. The house was sold. We moved to Kingston where my father took a new job, and we lived in an old farm house in the country. New everything—new school, community, friends, activities. It was there I had my first job, learned to drive, got my driver's license, went to my first prom, joined the church, belonged to a youth group, and won a public speaking prize. It was there I built a stone wall that's still standing, had a dog, milked goats, and raised chickens. But my father's job was in trouble. At the end of two years we moved back to Ottawa.

By an astounding coincidence, we actually bought back the very same house we had sold two and a half years earlier, but not before a vital delay. It might have been like the log returning to the same current I'd been in before leaving Ottawa, except for an amazing detour that changed my life forever.

When we returned to Ottawa, initially my parents could not find a house for sale that suited them. For five months we lived in a rented apartment at the corner of O'Connor and Cooper Streets in downtown Ottawa. Soon after moving in, I would wake up on Sunday mornings to the sounds of many people in motion. Across the corner was Chalmers United Church and people were streaming into its open doors. People of all ages—families with young children, teens in pairs or threes, retired people, graying executives or government officials, invalids in wheel chairs, older people with canes, single office girls, university students. Just before eleven the bells would peal, the last to arrive would hurry in through the still-open doors, and the massive sound of a thousand voices singing a swelling hymn of praise would claim my imagination. I had to see what this was about.

When I went I was soon captured by the gospel of Jesus Christ as preached by the young marvel, the Reverend A. Leonard Griffith, later to succeed Leslie Weatherhead at City Temple, London, England. I became a regular attendant. On weekdays all through my three years of undergraduate studies at Carleton University, I would have the lively stimulation and challenge of secular thought from the often humanist professors, and then on Sunday I would have my faith built up again by the magnificent Christian messages that poured with such power from the pulpit of Chalmers Church. It was there, at an E. Stanley Jones mission, that I accepted Christ as my Lord and Savior. It was that congregation that sponsored me when I felt my call to ministry and at that church that I preached my first sermon after my ordination.

This was but a link in the chain that led from my birth to my entering the ministry, but a vital link it was. And it was a detour. Strange indeed the ways of God. The Anglican Church that I sporadically attended with my father was only about four blocks from Chalmers, but I had never heard of Chalmers Church before moving in across the corner.

Our minds can rework it a thousand different ways: If we had remained in Ottawa and not been disrupted by moving away, I might never have known of this touch-point of God there in Chalmers Church. If my parents had directly contacted the owners of our former house and bought it back when we were first looking to relocate in Ottawa, I would likely have returned to the same dry and occasional church experience I had known previously. If we had found other accommodation than the corner of O'Connor and Cooper. If I had been skeptical and wary of the institutional church. If I had cynically said, "There are those hypocrites, singing out of one side of their sinful mouths again," and not gone across the corner. If my parents had pushed me to go, or worse yet had "dragged" me to go with them. If I had been too

shy and afraid of venturing into that strange new church alone …
the story of my life would have been dramatically different.

Or would it? Could God have not put someone else in my
path or warmed my heart over a Gideon Bible in a lonely hotel
room one night? Any detour will do, if God is there to meet you.

The Man

Mark* never thought he'd be in prison. Chalk it up to a
combination of stupidity and circumstance.

It all began with a drinking party. Because of the noise, the
police were called. They discovered that two of the women were
under age. No one, least of all Mark, had even imagined that.
"Thirty days."

While he was in jail, there was a riot and a guard was beaten
up. Mark had nothing to do with it, but he was slipped a threaten-
ing note: "Keep your mouth shut!"

With his silence, the authorities thought he was implicated.
"Two years."

Now he was mad. His stubbornness fought back. They tried
to break him. "Ninety days in the hole."

By the time he got out of the hole it was hate, and when he
was released from prison, he went on a rampage—violence, steal-
ing, you name it—and he was caught. "Two years."

So there he was in prison again, twenty-four, lonely, bitter,
and lost.

That's when the man started visiting him. He was a total stranger, part of a community program, just a Mennonite chicken farmer from the valley. He came every week and they soon became friends.

There in prison, with twenty-three other men on the tier with him, Mark had gotten used to the bragging and tall tales. "'Everyone has a million dollars, a Cadillac, and a blonde on the outside'—all fantasy. You get tired of the talk; but this guy was real."

The man would talk about his farm, his family, and his Amish lifestyle. He was so optimistic and cheerful. Mark thought, He doesn't drink or smoke or gamble. Boring! Yet he is happy as a lark. What makes this guy tick?

That's why Mark let him visit. This fellow had something Mark didn't have, and as Mark said, "He wasn't pushing religion at me."

Not that they didn't talk about deep things. Once Mark asked the man, "Where would I go if I died tonight?"

The man replied simply, "I don't know. It's not up to me to say."

The non-judgment in his answer felt good to Mark. Yet he knew the man was worried about Mark's future.

The visits continued for all of the time left in Mark's sentence. Then Mark lied about the actual date of his release. He didn't want the man to know. "I was scared—a fear of the unknown."

But as he walked out of prison that day, there was the man and the man's wife, waiting for him. "When I saw him standing there, I thought 'Oh, no! The last thing I want is religion.'"

What Mark really wanted was to go and get drunk and have some fun.

"He offered me a ride to the city—a free ride—so I accepted."

During the drive, the man said, "We'll have lunch here," and they stopped in a little town. Mark was wearing the suit he'd been issued in prison. He felt it marked him. Sensing his discomfort, the man took Mark to a menswear store after lunch and bought some street clothes for him.

When they were on the road again, the man said, "My farm is close by. Come in and see it."

While they walked through the barns and saw the set-up and the addition that was being put on, the man's wife was getting supper. "Stay for supper." Mark stayed.

Then it was getting dark. "Stay for the night."

"What made me say yes," Mark says now, "I'll never quite know; but I stayed."

After breakfast the next morning, he could see the carpenters at work on the addition to the barn. The man said, "Mark, there's a job here for you if you want, or I can drive you to the city. You decide." Mark stayed for six months.

After he'd been working on the farm for a week or so, it was time to get his stuff being kept by friends in the city. The man drove him there and dropped him off. This was what Mark had been waiting for. At his friends' place he had a couple of drinks. Some girls were there too. Mark went and sat in the corner. When the man came back for him, Mark got up and walked out. The man asked him simply, "Where do you want to go?"

Mark said, "Home."

After a month at the farm, Mark asked the man what "conversion" was.

"If you really ask God to forgive you, He will," was the answer.

Not a chance, thought Mark. "But one night when I was alone in the barn, I knelt down right there on the barn floor and asked God to forgive me for all the terrible things I had done. I was just so tired of the way I'd been living. I think that is all there was to it. Then, suddenly, it felt as if a thousand-pound sack was lifted off my back."

Other changes followed. Mark had smoked cigarettes since he was a kid. One evening after the forgiveness experience he prayed to be able to stop smoking. "I threw them away and have never touched them again or wanted to. If I was around people who were smoking, the smell would make me sick."

Working those six months for the man brought one amazing thing after another. For one thing, Mark could hardly believe how the man trusted him.

"He would give me the keys to the station wagon—me an ex-con. Every month he'd get checks of $12,000 or $13,000 from his chicken operation, and he'd send me into town to deposit them. Nobody had trusted me like that before."

It meant even more knowing that the man had tried to help others and had been burned by them more than once. One just took off with a truck and never came back.

That trust went even deeper than things did. A romance had developed between Mark and a girlfriend of the man's daughter.

Six months after Mark began working there, they were married. Today, after thirty-eight years together, they have three married sons and a daughter and nine grandchildren.

Before Mark had gone to jail, he had worked as a carpet layer. He had enjoyed that work and was good at it. Around the time of his wedding, while taking some things he had made in prison into a pawn shop to raise some money, Mark happened to see a complete set of carpet-laying tools there. "I bought them for next to nothing. It was an open door."

He went home and told his farmer-mentor that he wanted to go into business for himself. With the man's help he bought a van and set up shop as a carpet layer. He worked hard and earned good money. Within a year or two he had built a successful business and had two men working for him.

Success went to his head for a time though. It was easy to think, You've got it made! And that was a red flag. But Mark couldn't ignore God's voice in his heart: "Your pride is dangerous!" and heeded the warnings.

Shortly after, he sold the whole works and went on to other things. He bought a truck and hauled chickens for seven years. Then he and his wife bought five acres of land and developed that into a hobby farm. Soon they added a small egg operation.

The most significant changes have been spiritual. "I used to have a horrendous temper," Mark confided. "Jail didn't help. But that's all gone now. I just hand it over to God."

Knowing how he got sent to prison, you might imagine he would be miffed at the system. "No," he says. "I'm not offended at the law or the authorities, although it hasn't been easy at times. But if I hadn't gone to jail, I don't know where I'd be."

When he was in prison, Mark often dreamt of having a little house with a white picket fence, a wife, and children. Looking back, Mark says with a big grin, "I've got everything but the white picket fence."

All of the blessings in Mark's life began with the Mennonite chicken farmer. Now in his eighties, the man continues to be there for Mark. "He's like a father to me. If I have a problem, I can call him. He's such an amazing man. He just gives and gives and gives."

Soon after this story was written, the farmer died. Mark and his wife attended his funeral along with more than 300 others. One after another paid tribute to this man who had left such a legacy in their lives. They told of his inspiring example and the lasting influence of his faith and amazing kindness. As Mark's wife reflected later, "What came out time after time at the funeral was his gift of unconditional love."

Mark didn't speak at the funeral. The gratitude he felt would always be between himself, the man, and God.

Outwitting The Logical Mind

My friend Bert is a very bright guy. Now in his mid-seventies, he has spent most of his long career teaching students how to grasp some of the most intricate elements in the often-baffling world of computers. This is the story of how this electrical engineer, who was educated in the rather unspiritual world of modern technology, came to a personal faith in Christ. It was more than just a matter of convincing him of the reality of the Christian God; it was how to reveal that truth to him in such a way that he would not dismiss it as the trick of his own mind. That God knew just the right way to reach Bert is evident in what follows. Let him tell his own story:

It started in April 1962. On a cold, rainy night in Ottawa, I was talking to my friend, a professional engineer and research scientist. He was the first well-educated, scientifically-oriented Christian I had ever met. He had been guiding me for a while, giving me stuff to read. That night he changed gears. He asked me if I ever prayed. My quiet "no" was lost as he went on. "You can read all you want, but, if you don't pray, the faith will seem true on Mondays, Wednesdays, and Fridays—the other days of the week it won't." That was all he said.

I was sure that he would ask me sometime in the future whether I had started to pray. I was so intimidated by this that most mornings from then on before going to work I would recite the Apostles' Creed and the Lord's Prayer in the most mechanical way possible. Having been exposed to Anglicanism in my boyhood, this was the closest thing to prayer I could muster. So in any future confrontation I could tell him that I had started.

Gradually, I had a strange feeling that somehow I was starting to make progress. Like a sail boat in a very light wind, if you look ahead you don't see any change, but if you look behind, you can see ripples that prove you are moving.

In early August of that same year, at the end of an Anglican Communion Service, I decided to kneel in the pew and, in contrast to my previous efforts, to pray as hard as I could to God, if there was a God. My prayer was more or less wordless, but if I had used words I would have said, "This is me here. Are You out there somewhere?" It was my soul reaching out.

My next recollection is exploding into tears with such violence that the tears were splashed onto the inside of my glasses. I rose from my knees and in great chagrin looked around to see if there was anybody in the church. It was totally empty. When I stood up and walked in the aisle, I felt a strange lightness of my step, as though my full weight was not hitting the floor. I'm not a particularly emotional person and was embarrassed by this episode and could not account for it. I had not shed tears since childhood.

The next incident occurred about two weeks later. I experienced a most unusual mental shift that changed my life. I was having lunch at the St. Charles tavern on Queen Street and reading a Time magazine. In the Letters to the Editor section, a minister claimed that a previous article on the death of Marilyn Monroe had been excessively callous. At the Last Judgment, the minister said, we may all have to give an account for the destruction of this poor creature. I didn't know about the Last Judgment, but I found it odd that I had not seen through the article as clearly as the minister had. I glanced at the inset picture of Marilyn and realized that she was really quite beautiful.

I put the magazine down and looked at the wall. Then it hit me. It wasn't a vision in a physical sense—nothing I saw with my eyes. Instead, it was like my spirit becoming aware of two points of light—the one I "knew" represented the Father, the other the Son. Each was utterly distinct, yet they were simultaneously and completely unified. This is not a logical possibility in terms of the material world, but this is what my mind perceived. I knew in a way in which I had never known anything else that the Father and the Son exist, that they had always existed. No choir or angels. No ecstatic feelings. No emotion. Just the revelation of a simple, quiet fact. God is alive! I have never had a surprise like this before or since in my entire existence. I have never been so calm and elated, either. I became possessed of a kind of manic energy.

I left the restaurant and bumped into a naval officer whom I knew slightly from work. As I recall, I said something to him like, "I just saw God." He looked at me in a very startled way, obviously not knowing what to do with the intensity of my outburst, and said, "I'm a Baptist, and I go to church," as if to say, "Leave me alone." Within the next two days, a Muslim tennis friend suggested I see a psychologist!

Reflecting on this some weeks later with my Anglican priest, the Reverend Dr. Frank Uhlir, I asked why I had not seen three "lights" representing the Trinity. His reply paraphrased Jesus in John's Gospel: "When the Holy Spirit comes he will say nothing of himself but will speak only of me."[8] Sometime later I realized how significant seeing only the two lights truly was: had I seen three, I could have rationalized the vision away as some form of psychological projection of previous knowledge. Seeing two

---

8. Compare with John 15:26; 16:13, 14.

lights was nothing that I would have conjured up. For me it veri-
fied the divine origin of my vision, overriding the objections of
my logical mind.

In the days immediately following the tavern experience
I was a real nuisance to my friends. Some said that I didn't look
very well. I was becoming quite tired. I was beginning to realize
that I was in the grip of some kind of force from which I could
not break free. A week later, around noon, I realized that I had
been rereading the same paragraph in a book again and again
without being able to break the cycle. I then began to feel as if
there were two giant hands inside my rib cage pulling me apart.
I was terrified.

I ran out of the building to a public phone booth and
phoned Dr. Uhlir. I explained my predicament to him. He said,
"You must do exactly as I say. First, find a room where you can be
alone. You must pray for the forgiveness of all your sins. It does
not matter what sins you have committed. You must assume, re-
gardless of any feelings, that your sins have been forgiven. Then
you must call me."

Returning to my workplace, I went to the toilet, closed the
cubicle door, knelt on the floor with my face over the bowl, and
prayed for the forgiveness of my sins. At this point I must say I
had no idea what these sins might be and had little confidence
that prayer would work. I got up and felt a tremendous sense of
peace, peace like those very special moments in an Ottawa winter
when there is no wind and the snow falls in soft clumps, lighting
the whole city and descending with a quiet peace on everything.
With enormous relief, I now returned to the telephone booth

and reported these events to Dr. Uhlir. "Good," he said. "Keep in touch."

Some moments later I dialed a telephone number and my fingers went into the wrong holes (on the circular dial). No matter how hard I tried, I could not find the right holes. The force which had previously been tearing me apart had somehow returned, only in a more benign way. I did not have the terror as before but I could not dial a simple telephone number. Suspecting now that this was a spiritual problem, I again prayed for the forgiveness of my sins. I then dialed the number correctly and spoke to my friend.

An hour or two later, I was driving south on Elgin Street wanting to return to my apartment on Waverley. I became completely disoriented and could not determine whether I was going north or south on Elgin Street. There was no way I could find Waverley. There in the car I prayed again for the forgiveness of my sins. The next corner I came to was Waverley.

In this way my life continued until Saturday night, eleven days after the first episode in the tavern. Around 8:30 everything returned to normal—that is, to the ordinary way it had been before these amazing experiences of God. I had become used to and enjoyed the immediate sense of God's presence in my life and was adept at staying out of trouble. With this new turn of events, I now experienced a strong sense of disappointment and regret.

Once again I phoned Dr. Uhlir. I explained my return to "normalcy" and he said,

"This is perfectly natural. You could not have continued in this heightened spiritual intensity. It would have gradually destroyed you."

I asked him, "What do I do now?"

He answered with a question: "What have you learned?"

It was not difficult to answer: "To pray for the forgiveness of my sins."

"Continue to do so."

The next question I asked him was, "What will happen to me?"

He answered, "You will become one of the best teachers in your college."

This was prophetic. Near the end of my active career, nearly four decades later, I received an award for excellence in my teaching that year at the community college where I had spent most of my working life.

Those five months in 1962 of coming to faith changed my life. Previously, I had been driven by fear, specifically fear of failure. Life after high school had been a long and difficult struggle. I had wondered if I would ever find employment where I would be truly comfortable and at ease. Adding to those fears, in 1959 I had been fired from a job in Montreal. My confidence reached such a low ebb that I went to job interviews assuming that I wouldn't get the job. My inferiority complex was crippling me.

After this transformation, however, I could hear God saying in my head, "Stop apologizing for your existence. I made you. Do you think I don't know what I'm doing?" Having my self-confidence restored was the beginning of overcoming fear. Today I'm not afraid of any of the things that paralyzed me before the conversion. This elimination of fear and the increase in personal confidence, which continue to this day, were the greatest practical results of this dispensation of pure grace. It allowed me to eventually deploy the gifts God had given me and which fear had imprisoned for so long. I have experienced what Augustine meant when he said, "Become what you are."

In the four decades plus since that wonderful Tuesday in 1962, I have experienced the sheer practicality of living in God's presence, felt or assumed. For some believers, faith seems focused on some yet-to-be-realized future condition—"pie-in-the-sky-when-you-die." I don't say that this is bad. It is just that for me Christian belief is the most practical reality of living life fully now—like the well-operating tools of a carpenter. Almost as though the Christian faith is much more practical than it is "spiritual." I really live in a constant state of surprise.

What have I learned from it? That vision of the Trinity was the Saturn 5 that lifted me into an orbit I'm convinced I could not have entered in any other way. Yet many factors, some in long preparation, worked together with it to bring my faith to birth, including meeting a number of people in my late twenties who obviously had something that I lacked. Some of us believers who can trace our change to some brief period of time have had Saturn 5 moments. C.S. Lewis, for example, got on a bus a non-Christian and got off some minutes later a Christian. The "lift off" is very spectacular but not more important than the witness of people like Dr. Uhlir and my engineering friend, in my case, who were slowly building to the event.

I learned that God is living and powerful. Without these encounters, my religion would have been just a philosophy or moral guide. It would thus have been a religion of a dead god.

I discovered that God was not only living but capable of intervening in every element of my physical existence, any time He pleased.

Another thing I learned is that God is fearsome and can be terrifying if He so chooses. In coming to faith I nearly lost my mind. I also learned that if God chooses to withdraw His immediate presence, He can return anytime He wishes and only seems to be absent because He chooses to be so. Thus God is with us irrespective of how we feel.

Most amazing of all for me was how in the twinkling of an eye my scientific, super-intellectual control of everything was bypassed by a vision so simple yet so compelling that it brought me face to face with the truth of God. No day has since passed when I do not recall that vision.

MOMENTS THAT CONVINCE & SHAPE US

What exactly creates our faith in God? These days the nature-nurture debate is pretty much an academic question: whether heredity or education, in its broadest sense, is more influential is a moot point. Whatever we might be born with, when it comes to faith, surely it is our experience that wins the day. "Give me a child until he is five," it has been said, "and I will have him for the rest of his life."

When we look back on our lives, each of us can identify several key experiences that determined how we came to view ourselves, our world, and God. They were what could be called "moments that convince and shape us." Some may recall a confrontation when there was a struggle of wills. You wanted what you wanted. Your father or mother drew the line: "no." Your eyes met, and forever after you had that view of authority, for good or ill. Another person will remember the loving arms of a mother who scooped him or her up from a painful accident and held him or her close. These were decisive moments. Although intellectual reasons may have some effect, the more emotional experiences, coming earlier, likely play a more crucial role in setting the tone toward a positive or negative faith outlook for the rest of our lives.

What then are we to make of lives that run counter to this pattern? When negative influences fail to have negative effects, and when early tragic losses do not create despair or turn a person against God, what then? Are we thrown back on heredity to explain it, or is there something else at work?

In the two stories that follow, we might have expected an angry response to life, even rebellion against God, or atheism or despair; instead we find faith. The third story, "A Sign in Time," is about a special kind of "convincing"—the kind that turns the fierceness of temptation aside and puts our feet on the path to life.

‖‖‖

Love Made All The Difference

At eighty, my friend Kurt* was reflecting on his early life. "I assumed there was a God. But he was a mixed up God. I was really an agnostic."

There was ample reason for his doubts. The first fifteen years of his life were marked by just one setback after another.

"God kept dealing me cards off the bottom of the deck," he said. "There was a whole sequence of unfortunate events over which I had no control." It had been difficult to say the very least.

Born in 1928 in Pennsylvania to a Polish father and French Canadian mother, he was soon plunged with his family into the Great Depression. One day, when his unemployed father was out looking for work, he was hit and instantly killed by a truck. Kurt was four. He had a sister, age three, and a baby brother. Their mother was distraught. Kurt was separated from his sister and sent to live with his father's mother.

Two years later, when he was six, his grandmother died. Kurt found her on the floor. Not knowing what to do, he went over to a nearby store and told them his grandmother had died. He recalls them saying, "You need a coroner."

"No, I need a doctor," Kurt replied. He thought that death was temporary and that both his grandparents would come back with presents. His imagination was trying desperately to make up for the harshness of reality. Shortly afterward, he and his sister were placed with foster parents.

When he was eight, he went to live with his mother's parents in a small town in Ontario. Within a year both of these grandparents died and Kurt's mother came to claim him and his sister.

Looking back now, Kurt says, "God must have a sense of humor. He seems to have been saying, 'I'm not finished with you yet; you will have to suffer more so that you will appreciate the good I will do for you.'"

Adversity became his motivator. Kurt thought, If no one will help me, I'll have to do something for myself.

He became interested in a variety of subjects, far beyond his years. "I went to the library and asked the librarian for books on mythology, history, literature—not religion because I didn't like God."

He plunged into books, reading Goethe, de Maupassant, and classics of all kinds. He was nine! Books were his passion, but it was not books that brought him to faith in God.

He remembers coming home after school one day to find the house deserted. His mother had just walked out and abandoned them. They then went to live with his aunt and uncle. So it was at eleven years of age that he was told by his uncle that he would have to support himself. It was decided that he would complete his education to the end of high school and pay his way by working in his uncle's store. Up at dawn, he would open the store and work there until it was time for school; then after school it was back to the store and work until closing.

He remembers saying to himself, "Here I am, eleven years old and going nowhere." Now he says, "I used to look at other kids in my class who had a home, loving parents, and it seemed a dream that would never come true."

When he was twelve, he formed a great admiration for Albert Schweitzer. Partly it was because of Schweitzer's German language. Kurt had learned German from his foster parents and his father; it was a language he dearly loved and to which he felt such a deep emotional connection. Then partly it was because of Schweitzer's prodigious talents and his profound humanitarian service.

"I admired that he was so versatile—philosopher, physician, theologian, musician—and that he gave it all up to serve humanity in Africa. He was my hero."

Yet it was not Schweitzer who brought him to faith in God.

Meanwhile, both his uncle and aunt seemed to take their anger with his mother out on him. He developed a deep resentment toward his uncle, who made life miserable for him in the store. But he had no choice and no way to vent his anger. People in town came to know the unfairness of this system. He was a good student and good in sports and found some consolation in the popularity he enjoyed. Downtrodden at home, he received a lot of support and encouragement from others.

When he was seventeen and finishing high school, two townspeople drove him for an interview to apply to the university in a nearby city. His aunt and uncle had forbidden him to go beyond high school, but he went for the interview anyway. As punishment, his uncle locked him out for the night before his trig exam. Kurt's dander was up.

"I'll show him," he said to himself. He wrote the exam and got one hundred percent.

Without a cent from them, Kurt went to the university and graduated, all without any debt. Scholarships and hard work paid the way. After graduating, he went to Switzerland to do further study. Because of his family and foster family background, he could speak German, French, and English, as well as some Spanish and Italian, all of which stood him in good stead in Switzerland.

At the university he was directed to a family where he could live. The lodgings were small and uninviting, the family situation difficult, and the woman of the house could only provide him with breakfast, but something made him say yes. It was perhaps the most important decision of his life.

Up to that point Kurt had had little or no reason to believe in God's goodness. What he had achieved was his own doing. From the many hard knocks he had received, God would have seemed a hard and punishing God, "dealing off the bottom of the deck," as Kurt said. But there in Switzerland God intervened.

In Kurt's own words: "The first real sign of this woman's true character came when I had only been in her home for about three months. I was playing hockey for Zurich and was on my way there after classes. I took a shortcut through a disused building and was right in the middle when it collapsed. There were spectators; the city hall was notified and rescue operations took two hours. They fully expected to find me dead, but, miracle of miracles, I had no life-threatening injuries. I did have to spend six weeks in the hospital while injuries to my spine, which proved temporary, were allowed to heal. What did this woman do? She came every afternoon for the entire six weeks to visit me. Remember that she had a handicapped family and did not drive. This meant two to three hours out of every busy day. I was totally astounded! Never in my life had anybody cared so much about me. First this miracle and then a profound example of love, motivated by her Christian faith. 'It is what God would want me to do,' she said simply when I asked her about it. Was this the same God, I wondered, who had let me down so many times?"

Over the next five years he became part of that family. The woman had many hardships. After marrying and having three children, she had discovered that her husband had a degenerative disease, which their children would get. The husband died during the first year Kurt was there and her seventeen-year-old son died during the second year. But Kurt was there to console her. No doubt because of his own griefs, he felt compassion for her and wanted to do something for her. Instead he was blessed by her. What he saw in her response was "unbelievable." Despite these blows, she didn't give up on God. She was a very devout Catholic and attended church on a daily basis. Because of her faith, she simply didn't let these things get her down. It made a deep impression on him.

Kurt was there for two years. Then he was away, first in Canada establishing his career, then traveling and consulting, doing refugee work in Vienna and elsewhere. Whenever possible on his travels, he would visit her. When he saw her in 1956, she made a pact with him. She needed a son and he needed a mother.

"For the rest of her life she was that to me." From then on he called her "mother." Knowing her, he made a huge discovery: "She really loved people. She was the epitome of love."

In 1959, he went back and saw her again on his way to Russia, and it was the same. "Here is this person who loves me, who devotes herself to me."

It changed his life. Previously he had felt sorry for himself. Now he had someone to care for. His selfishness melted away.

"Before that I couldn't see myself getting married." But now he could and he did. Also, he committed to support a foster child and visited her in Naples.

And his faith? "Any semblance of Christianity before was very superficial," he admitted. Now he knew God in his heart.

"I saw what God could do with people who had faith in Him. There was always my mother's love to show the way. I felt a security I had never felt before."

One day Kurt decided to honor her before she died.

"With the help of the university president I set up a special fund in her name. The university honored her publicly. As I could not be there, I taped a message in German and had it read at the ceremony. My mother cried for joy. I honestly felt it was God that had inspired me to do this."

Today, at eighty-two, he still has a lively faith in God, is certain of God's goodness and love, and has served many years as a church elder. Looking back, he can say he is thankful for God's many mercies through his life.

"Where would I be if I'd had a perfect life? Nowhere near what I have accomplished and done," he says. He's traveled widely in the service of government and humanitarian causes, helped relocate refugees after the Hungarian Revolution, taught at a university, and written a weekly column for over forty years. He still works as a media analyst, features writer, and consultant. He has a loving wife, two grown children, and two grandchildren.

This is his testament of that woman's influence on him: "As a result of many years of benefiting from her love that she had both for me and for mankind in general, I gradually began to understand better what God's love was all about. If I didn't love my neighbor, how could I ever hope to love myself? God projects His love through us. She was a perfect example of this. I didn't feel that I could ever match her, but I became convinced that her approach was the right path to follow. She praised me when I did something well; she never criticized, only suggested. It was a joy to go back 'home' to Switzerland. My only regret was that she was so far away most of the time. I tried whenever I could to show her my love for her. We might be separated in denomination but not by Christian love."

Humanly, there seems no way to balance the losses and hardships in this man's experience, especially in his early life, in order to account for his faith. The blows he received would have overwhelmed most people. Yet against all those negatives is set the simple goodness, faith, and love of that one woman, his "mother." Her love won out.

A Persistent Goodness

A child knows when something is wrong; but sometimes it takes years, even a lifetime, to understand what it was. Trish's first memories were confusing and unhappy: images of a small house with only a kitchen and two bedrooms. Her mom and dad's bedroom was very tidy and off-limits to the kids. The children's bedroom was very untidy, filled with boxes and sleeping places and clutter. She was somewhere between three and four.

About that same time she recalls her father coming home with candies and giving some to her and her twin sister. She can't recall exactly what happened after that, only that something wasn't right. In another scene her father is crouching unsteadily in front of her baby brother and saying, "Hit me."

She thought, Norman★ doesn't understand; he's only a baby. He was hardly two.

Just last year, more than sixty years later, her older sister explained what had happened: their father had hit Norman and knocked him down. Her sister thought he was trying to teach Norman how to fight like a man!

Much of Trish's confusion centered on her father. She feared him and turned inward. She remembers the time when he told her gruffly to use her right hand for eating. His tone paralyzed her. She was only three and didn't know right from left. But her mother came to the rescue. Trish and the younger children ate on a table attached to the wall. On the one side were shelves covered with a curtain. In the tenseness of the moment, her mother walked behind them and said in a hushed voice, "It's your hand next to the curtain." She still recalls the comfort she felt from her mother's voice.

She also remembers the sound of running feet outside the house and being afraid. There was something terrifying about going behind the house.

The reality behind these images is that hardship had overshadowed Trish's life right from the beginning. Her twin sister was born with a broken hip and she herself was thought to be dead. But they both survived as members of a dirt-poor family, with two more yet to be born. They lived in a three-room tar paper shack in the back woods.

During the Depression, her father became an alcoholic and would come home drunk and abusive. To protect them, her mother would sometimes send the children outside to hide. Trish would huddle in her hiding place outside, trembling in fear. She was well hidden, but her sister would stand up and demand to know why their mother had sent them outside, putting them all in danger.

There was a terrible night when she was four. She remembers being ushered out of the house in the dark. "Dad was sitting in a chair by the table, in front of the window. We were taken to our nearest neighbor. Later that night, we were in a big car, driving through the night. It was a very dark night and I had scary dreams. It turned out that we were taken to our grandfather's home. The house was big with many rooms and dark wood paneling. We had never seen such a fine place. But Grandpa was grumpy."

In the days that followed, they had fun playing in his maple bush and beating on a galvanized tub. But all was not well. One day in a nearby park she overheard whispering. "There's that family. It's them!" She knew that they were talking about her family.

Abuse comes in various shades and colors. Physical violence and sexual invasion are recognized for their intensity, while the stigma of shaming has more subtle shades. Being labeled and talked about like that in the park inflicted considerable damage. But the emotional pain of having an unpredictable father who repeatedly betrayed your trust and the anguish of seeing your father possessed by booze and your mother battling to protect her children marked her soul for life. How the world of children is shattered when their parents' lives crumble before their eyes.

In Trish's world, matters had come violently to a head between her parents. Years later Trish learned the truth from her mother. Her father's threats and abuse had become totally monstrous. He was planning to teach Trish's older sisters how to have sex; he and Trish's mom would show them! Her mother had to stop him. She shot him dead. What Trish had seen that night was her father sitting up in the chair with a bullet hole through his chest.

Her mother turned herself and the gun in to police and was charged with murder. The effect on Trish's mother was beyond words. Her life had been shattered and was now in grave danger. She could not eat. She hardly slept. She was sure she would die there in jail. In the midst of that desperate situation, an unseen voice said to her, "Sally★, eat your food." Falling to her knees, she prayed to God to save her and promised she would raise her children to know Him.

Public pressure mounted in her support. Money came from near and far. Strangers became allies and advocates. The charge was reduced to manslaughter. She escaped the death penalty on compassionate grounds that she had acted to save her children. The younger children including Trish went to live with various relatives until their mother completed her sentence and could gather them together again and make a home.

Sometime later, using the money that had been donated, her mother was able to purchase a larger house and begin to re-build their family life. Trish remembers how on Sunday mornings her mother would take them to church in the little schoolhouse when there were services there. A couple of summers, traveling missionaries came to teach the children about Jesus. That was the first of their Christian education.

One can hardly imagine the emotional scars such a beginning would leave on Trish and her siblings. Her young life was haunted by insecurity and marked by the stigmas of poverty and the murder. How could one hope to find peace or healing for such memories, or to salvage an intact life out of such chaos?

Certainly in the years that followed one can see the dire effects of these early circumstances. Coming out of high school she planned to study music, but her emotional needs got in the way. Pursuing her relationship with her boyfriend took precedence. No doubt it was searching for love and belonging that led to her becoming pregnant and marrying him at seventeen. Her dream of a career in music was put on hold. Instead she was saddled with the adult responsibilities of making a home and caring for what would soon be two children. She tried to make the best of it. They moved to a larger house in the country, which was remote. On Sundays they went to church, but she became tired of going to all the trouble of getting ready and trying to make the children look decent. People didn't talk to them and she got nothing out of the service. They soon stopped going to church.

As life unfolded so cruelly for her, there was, at the same time, the hint of a positive force at work. During this time she first became aware of something that seemed like God. She was part of a singing group and whenever they would go into a church to sing, she would cry. She didn't know why, only that it felt good. She thought many times about those tears and came to realize that it was God nudging her and saying, "You've had a very hard life. But I haven't let go of you." Some years later a Christian woman confirmed the positive of these tears when she told Trish, "It was a gift."

She would need all the positives she could find to make her marriage work. The attitudes and experiences she had learned in her family of origin had not prepared her for the challenges of marriage but instead proved to be a handicap. Trish and her husband tried valiantly at first but soon encountered crosscurrents and mounting difficulties. After four years, their marriage deteriorated into a loveless stalemate. They could work together and they could parent together, but they could not be intimate. From early in their marriage, sex had been a problem for her. She could not relax in the sexual relationship but felt that someone was always watching from the upper corner of the bedroom. Soon she could not tolerate him to touch her. In turn, he accused her of being frigid. When the children were old enough, she got a job, which gave her a life away from her husband. But he felt threatened by anything that took her away from him. He wanted to do everything together; she felt stifled by that. The gulf between them widened. She went out more on her own. Finally, to prove as much to herself as to him that she was not frigid, she had an affair. That only made her feel more self-loathing. They went to counseling, but both of them walked out terribly disappointed with the counselor.

It is an extreme situation when a mother leaves her children, for any reason. That Trish left home alone several times shows just how serious the problems were. But she always came back because of the children. After twelve or thirteen years of this, she and her husband made an agreement to give it one last try. She would stay for at least three years more to prepare the children as best she could for life, and after that, if the situation didn't improve, she would leave for good. They both tried for almost three years, but it was tearing her apart. At one point she was so emotionally frazzled that she couldn't even stand to touch her one hand to the other. She was so miserable and depressed that she was certain she would die unless she left her marriage. Finally, she summoned up the strength and left.

She got a small apartment and lived alone for one year. It was then that her dreams began to speak to her in earnest. One of the most powerful was of being slowly electrocuted seated to a table at her workplace. "I knew I was going to die. I realized I have one hope. God can save me. Great light shone all around, and I was released from the electricity coming through the table. I was able to move my hands."

The relief was palpable. As a result of this dream, she told herself, "I'm going to live by praying to God." This was typical of what she called "disaster dreams" that occurred through this time in her life. Something terrible would threaten her life, but then the dream would always end on a note of hope.

In another such dream, "a long, wide crack appeared on the ground in front of me. The ground was of cement and had looked barren before, but now it was terrifying. Suddenly a message filled the air, 'Run for your life. Rape and plunder.' Fear moved my feet as my mind searched for where I had left the car. Where was it? Running madly, I finally found the car but it would not start. Keep running! But to where? Spying a phone booth, I dialed the police. They could not help. I kept running and saw several more phones but could not stop because men were chasing me. I had to get home. The road before me suddenly changed and became a road I used as a child when I went home from school. However, instead of a friendly passage, it was now an obstacle course, filled with tall, pointed rocks. I would have to jump from one to another to get down the hill. Scared of falling hundreds of feet, I began the descent. Then, far below, I saw a man leaping easily from one peak to another. He jumped without fear and had no trouble. I realized that he was giving me an example to follow. I concluded, 'Don't be afraid. You'll be safe.' I woke up and knew it was Jesus."

It is interesting that, although she did not have any outward religious practice at the time, somewhere in her unconscious there was spiritual power and presence.

Soon afterward she began a serious relationship with a nother man which lasted for twelve years. They had only lived together for little more than a year when she found a lump on her throat and was diagnosed with Hodgkin's Lymphoma. Just a few months before she discovered the lump, she had dreamed of a train coming in a circle on the water and laying a track behind it as it came. Holding the train up at the front was a big rock under the engine. "When I woke up I thought, That was God, the Rock of Salvation." This was at a time before the lump was discovered when she would wake up at night with major sweats.

Three months of tests followed which confirmed the lymphoma to be in stage three of four. She knew her life was in grave danger. She began to think more about God and bought a Bible. A series of treatments was carried out over the winter months. Some were very difficult and tiring for her, but she persevered.

The following spring she felt the need to be alone. The world of nature had always been a refuge for her and now she had a strong urge to go into nature and be comforted. She took the day off and went to a small, scrawny area of bush near a major intersection.

"I found a dry spot under a relatively large tree and lay my jacket on the ground. Lying down, I rested and slept lightly. After a time I went home, refreshed and able to carry on."

In the summer that followed, there were modest signs of improvement. She recorded three dreams which had positive symbols that encouraged her—of the replacement of body parts, of floating in clear, clean water, and of lying deep in water in a fetal position. They all were accompanied with feelings of comfort and wellbeing.

"A few months later I was told my cancer was in remission. As I looked back I realized that I had been given a gift. Having cancer caused me to examine my physical and spiritual life. In the years that followed I did just that, but not immediately."

Three years after treatment was finished, she had one particular dream that seemed to speak of an important closure: "I was in a rowboat rowing across the waters. There had been five small stones in the bottom of the boat. They were in my keeping. But I lost them. I had to make the confession that I had lost them. As I approached the shore, there was a fisherman sitting by the edge of the water, fishing. I told him that I had lost the stones. He let me know that it was okay. He invited me to look around. So I walked around the shore and looked into the clear water. And guess what—there were thousands of stones! I felt that I was forgiven and given another chance. When I woke up I was certain that that fisherman was Jesus."

Outwardly there was no evidence of these inner encounters with God. For twelve years she lived a very secular lifestyle with this man. But gradually she realized that the differences in their values had created a great gulf between them, and she left.

"Soon after, I felt a yearning to find a church," she says. "I was living alone at that time. I started to go to church."

There she was surprised to discover how much she needed the Word of God.

"It seemed that everything the minister had to say was pointed at my life. As I heard God's Word in the preaching and in the scripture readings, I realized how far I had wandered away. The desire grew strong within me to reconnect with God and to live the kind of life He would want."

In a quiet time one day she recommitted her life to the Lord. Soon she found herself making some significant life changes. "I gave up my Saturday night entertainment to get up and go to church Sunday morning and sing in the choir." Later she joined a Bible study group and was active in her church's community outreach to those who were poor, disabled, or unemployed.

"It was then that I could see that God had never left me. Looking back, I realized that those dreams had been given so that I could handle the cancer. I'd been led to that church so I could have a closer walk with God."

Even her jumble of difficult and trying experiences right from childhood on had been shaped through suffering, patience, and faith for a good purpose.

"I'm still struggling," she says, "but I've learned that God is always there to help. Like those tears in church, He's been nudging me all my life. I just paid less attention to Him than He did to me. God doesn't let go of you."

It does appear that in strange and often unlikely ways, her mother's pledge to God made there in prison—the pledge to raise her children to know God—is being fulfilled.

A Sign In Time

Ted★ was exhausted as he walked back to his room. Conventions always wore him down. He could only take so many speakers, charts, statistics, panel discussions, and focus groups before details blurred over. At least it would be over tomorrow and he would fly home.

Tonight, the last night of the convention, had been set as free time. Rounding the last bend in the corridor before his room, he considered the possibilities. He was tired and could just relax, watch some TV, and turn in early. He had turned down an invitation to go out on the town with the guys because he just wanted to be alone and quiet for a change. But secretly he had entertained a fantasy of seeking out a woman companion for the night. The thought gave him energy but it also brought fear and shame. What was he thinking? He was a family man. He and Barb had been married twelve years and had two lovely children. He had never cheated on her.

He put the thought aside as he slipped the card in the key slot and pushed the door open. The cool room felt good as he eased his shoes off and undressed to have a shower. In the community and workplace he was a model of responsibility, a hardworking professional, a regular churchgoer, an active member in his service club, and a coach in little league. It was totally out of character for him to consider sacrificing his honor and decency. For years he had given and served others, without regret. Why stop now?

But as he stepped into the hot shower, he realized that duty and dedication were beginning to wear thin. He was unhappy. The tiredness was not just physical; it was emotional and spiritual. All his effort and loyalty were not bringing him the satisfaction and recognition he needed. Earlier he could always convince himself things would improve, that his sacrifices would be rewarded, but now in midlife he was beginning to think more of himself. If he were brutally honest, he would have to confess that he believed that life owed him more than he was receiving, especially in marriage. To him it seemed a one-way street in which he was always giving and she was always too tired or not interested in him. The times of intimacy were long past. Though he was still attentive and tried his best to be patient, he concluded that she either did not understand him and his needs or that she didn't care. Whoa! Enough of that, he told himself. Self pity! Let it go. Turning the shower off he dried and dressed for dinner.

Soon he was sitting by himself at a nearby restaurant enjoying a steak. But the mood returned, this time with urgency and desire. It had been over two months since they had made love. He was a red-blooded man; right or wrong, it just wasn't fair that his wife would be so cold and disinterested. He needed affection, both to give and to receive. After paying the bill, he went out into the street.

It was early evening, and the sinking sun put a red glare on the store windows he passed. It would soon be dark. He was charged with curiosity and the excitement of whom he might meet. All thoughts of shame and decency had been lost somewhere under the surging tide of desire. He wasn't quite sure what he might do if the opportunity of an encounter presented itself, but his plan was to explore the possibility.

In the distance up the street he could see the bright lights beginning to glisten as darkness grew deeper. A few people were walking on the street, and cars were slowly passing. He caught the eye of one or two women drivers, and the thought of one of them stopping inflamed him. But they kept on going. Ahead he saw a corner bar with its beer light flashing. A young woman in shorts and high heels walked with a suggestive wiggle toward it only to be met by a black man with dread knots who had been waiting against the storefront. Together they went in its front door. Ted contented himself with the assurance that there would be other bars ahead and the night was still young. How he longed for companionship and an understanding and willing partner.

As he strode further into the night along the street, the debate revived weakly within him of guilt over what he was doing, but it was no match for the sinful desires that flooded him. He was almost abandoned to it and ready to accept any offer when he noticed that the building beside him was a church—one of those "blood of the Lamb" type churches he had never been attracted to. There on the scant lawn stood the church's sign shining its black and white message into the night: "Every way of a man is right in his own eyes, but the Lord weighs the heart. Proverbs 21:2." Ted knew without a doubt those words were for him.

His pride kept him walking slowly to the corner so that no one would suspect the truth. But there were tears in his eyes. The decision had been made the moment he read the words. His ordeal was over. As he turned and took his first steps back, his heart fairly exploded with joy. He was going home.

PHYSICAL DELIVERANCE

Nowhere is God's intervention more evident than in miraculous escapes from harm or almost certain death. Natural forces had been set in motion. The person was caught, whether by foolishness, error, or circumstance, in the direct line of danger that threatened to take his or her life. It seemed inevitable, except … something or Someone intervened.

"Get Out. Get Out Now!"

The cottage was a sanctuary for Ian.★ Nestled there by the lake, it was a place of refuge where he and Cynthia★ could escape the heat of the city in the summer. He loved the smell of the woods, the clean air in the highlands, the water, and the beach. The natural rhythms of earth, sky, and water soon relaxed and unwound the tensions of the city-dweller.

Ian needed to relax. His job as a police officer kept him constantly on his toes. Even at home when he slept, a note of vigilance was always sounding in the background. He enjoyed police work and was well-suited to it. It satisfied his twin nature—action and serving. He was physical—a muscular six-footer who needed to be doing—and he was spiritual—a man of deep Christian faith who cared. In his ten-year career he had an outstanding record of both leadership and service that went far beyond the call of duty. Seeing a need and an opportunity, he had set up the Fellowship of Christian Peace Officers across Canada. Yes, his work was fulfilling and he needed some restful time to recharge his energy.

The cottage belonged to Sid★, his father-in-law. Ian and Cynthia had been coming up whenever they could in the summers for the eight years of their marriage. On this particular three-day weekend Ian wasn't going to get much rest, however. Some major work had to be done on the cottage, and when your father-in-law asks for help, you pitch in.

The cottage was really little more than a frame box, twenty-four by thirty-six feet. To extend its usefulness, the family decided to insulate it. The first phase was to wrap the water pipes and insulate the floor from beneath. That involved jacking the whole building up so that they could do the necessary work underneath it. Ian's brother-in-law, Greg★, who was a heating and air conditioning contractor, would be in charge with Sid and Ian as crew.

When it dawned as a bright and sunny day on Saturday they made an early start. The cottage sat on three 8 by 12 inch beams that ran the thirty-six-foot length of the building. The beams themselves were supported by eight-inch cement blocks, spaced evenly throughout the length of the beams. Sid had purchased twelve five-ton hydraulic jacks, four for each beam. The men set about putting the jacks in place evenly under each beam and snugging them up until they were almost weight-bearing. Greg had improvised a leveling device from a long piece of hose stretched from one side of the cottage to the other. By filling it with water and marking the water levels at each end, he could tell when the building was level as they began to jack it up.

Ian volunteered to crawl under the cottage and operate the four jacks supporting the middle beam. Sid took the outside beam on the south side, and Greg the one on the north. Ian didn't mind being under the cottage in the least. It was a hot and oppressively humid day. No one wanted to be in the full sun and it was cooler in the shade under the cottage. As he crawled under he could see the open space to the far end. The ground was uneven in places, but he was able to get by with inches to spare between himself and the floor above. He made one complete sweep of the pathway he would be crawling on beside the beam, clearing away pebbles, sticks, and cobwebs. Then he was ready and he called to Greg to begin.

It was slow and tedious work, ratcheting one jack one or two clicks, then another jack, then another, until all twelve jacks on all three beams had been raised. There was much calling back and forth between them to coordinate the lifting. Most of the time Ian was just lying there while the outside beams were being raised their one or two clicks. So he went and got a book to read and crawled back under the cottage again. It was cool and fairly comfortable there and he was able to read between his times of responsibility. At one point he couldn't believe his ears. Above him he could hear sounds of movement in the cottage. One or two family members had entered and were walking around. He told them plainly to get out. Things then returned to normal, none the worse for the interruption.

The lifting process was progressing well, though agonizingly slowly. Greg was being extra careful, which added to the time. All of the jacks had been raised in succession at least ten times and they would soon have enough space to insert a second concrete block at each support place. They would just need another round of ratcheting to reach the necessary height.

Ian was lying on his side reading his book while the others were working on their jacks when he heard the words, "Get out. Get out now!" At first he thought the voice was outside himself. Then he realized no one else could hear it. It was inside his head, in his right ear.

The words were so clear and distinct they immediately got his attention. "What?" he thought to himself.

It came a second time. "Get out. Get out now!"

With that, he was seized with terror. He now realized he was in immanent danger. Dropping his book, in one motion he rolled over and crawled out on his belly like a snake as fast as he could. Just as he got to his feet, the whole cottage slid forward off the jacks and fell with a terrible crash almost two feet to the ground. Greg and Sid came running from the sides of the cottage. Sid was screaming, "Ian! Ian!"

When they saw he was okay, they said almost simultaneously, "We thought you were dead. Thank God, you're okay."

"Yes, thank you, Lord," echoed Ian.

He was badly shaken, as they all were. As they dusted Ian off, Greg apologized again and again. Then they sat down and caught their breath. Afterward they inspected the damage. Everything loose in the cottage had fallen. It was quite a mess. Food had spilled out of the refrigerator. Plates, cups, and dishes were strewn on the floor. Most breakables were smashed.

Damage to the cottage itself was only minor, but the edges of some of the beams were splintered by glancing blows off of some blocks as it fell. Somehow the beams missed directly hitting any of the existing concrete blocks and landed flat on the ground with no clearance whatever. If Ian had not gotten out, he would certainly have been crushed to death.

None of them had any heart to continue that day. Later in the weekend, when they did take up the repair job, they decided just to restore the cottage to its original single block support system, the way it had been. In the years following, the cottage never did get insulated.

What came from all of that effort were the life lessons learned. For Ian it was the clear message that our lives are in God's hands: "For the Lord to actually audibly warn me to escape such a horrible death means He must have a plan and purpose for my life."

Breakpoint Faith

Two friends and I were discussing how God had become real in our lives. Bob was a retired social services administrator with a strong military background and training. John was a retired airline pilot with a long and distinguished career. Beginning in the Royal Canadian Air Force, he then served as a pilot for nearly thirty-three years for two major commercial airlines, flying on many international routes on five continents.

Each of us had been raised in church-related families and had been taught the Christian faith from childhood. We knew many of the arguments for God's existence and could talk about God, but we wanted to go deeper and hear what actual experiences had helped shape our personal faith in God.

As we talked, it soon became clear that holding onto control had been a central issue for each of us. It had actually kept us from trusting God. We admitted that trying to manage everything ourselves had often prevented us from asking God for guidance or from the possibility of ever seeing God's power in action. Along the way, we kidded about how foolish we humans are when we think we can master life with its huge challenges without trusting in God.

John mentioned that for airline pilots, of course, control is an absolute necessity. Pilots are taught to have control at all times and in every detail. In some ways this emphasis on control had made it harder for him to let go to God in faith. Then he told us the following story to show how God got his attention and helped establish his faith.

Early in his flying career, when he was full of youthful bravado, he was trying out a jet over the Chatham area of New Brunswick, Canada. He spotted a railroad crew working on the track below and thought he'd push the limits and give them a thrill. Diving at them, he made a few fast passes. The standard rule was not to go below five hundred feet, but he passed below that.

Then he decided on a whim to give them a final scare before leaving. Taking the jet up to a peak, he rolled into another steep dive toward the men on the track. Somewhat mesmerized by his last "strafing" run, he delayed his pullout until he suddenly realized that he was very, very low. He rapidly pulled back and the plane immediately began to "judder," a symptom of a high-speed stall as the airflow broke away from the main wing and buffeted the tail of the plane. He knew from his training that when it did that the pilot had less and less control. As he tried desperately to balance the "G" force required to stop the descent without increasing the juddering, he thought, I may not be able to pull out of this. It may all be over.

Then he had a sensation of intense heat coming up from his feet and seat to the top of his head. Fear. As he did his utmost to pull out, the dive angle was decreasing, but the rate of descent was just too great. He knew he was helpless: he couldn't do enough to avoid hitting the ground. Now he was certain he was going to die. I've really done it this time, he thought.

For a split second, at the very bottom of the dive, he lost all sense of what happened. Later he calculated that almost certainly he had gone below the tree line, just feet from the ground. How he missed hitting the trees amazed him. But the next thing he knew he was flying a smooth course safely above the earth. To this day he doesn't understand what happened. He had gone outside the envelope of reasonable maneuvering—and survived. That day he found that when he was out of control, God took a hand to manage the situation and to save his life.

Such a near-death experience could not help but have a profound effect on him. Immediately he had an exhilarating sense of how fortunate he was to be alive. From then on, he would cherish life as never before. This episode also became a point of reference for his whole flying career. Overnight he developed a highly cautious and mature attitude in all the details and decisions he made in flying. Ironically, he became safety officer for his squadron and later spent five years as an instructor—a job which he regarded as his highest contribution to flight safety. Ever since, whenever he hears of an accident or mishap, John says to himself, "There, but for the grace of God, go I." He knows that when he has done his best he can trust the rest to God.

"A Golden Light ... And Peace"

Premonitions can be really scary. Tracy Praill, thirty-three, had one as she was driving over the Ambassador Bridge to pick up her six-year-old son and his babysitter at the Detroit Metro Airport. It was September 14, 2000. They were gathering for her brother's wedding to be held two days later across the river in Windsor, Ontario. While on the bridge she had a strong sense that she was going to be in a car accident. The unsettling thought made her slow down. One of her childhood fears was of driving off a bridge into water. She wasn't a strong swimmer.

"I couldn't shake it. I thought, How terrible to have an accident here on the bridge and go over the side into the water."

The fear became so strong that Tracy reached out in desperation and prayed: "God, if I have to be in an accident, I don't care about the vehicle. It's just a possession. But I don't want to die, and please don't let me hurt anybody." She cleared customs and drove on more slowly than normally.

The roads in downtown Detroit can be confusing for a stranger. She became lost in a run-down neighborhood and had to ask directions. Then a man driving beside her opened his window and said "something's wrong with your back tire." She pulled over and checked but could see nothing amiss. She drove on. Tracy then found herself at the wrong airport and had to go back and get on the thruway that would take her to the Metro Airport. All the while the sense of foreboding clung to her and she drove cautiously in the slow lane. Fortunately the road was dry and the visibility was good. At last she could see the planes landing and taking off in the distance.

"I thought, This is crazy. I can see the airport. I'm fine. Nothing has happened." So she went from the slow lane to the middle lane to the fast lane.

It was rush hour now. Everybody was coming off work. All around her the cars were driving quickly. She was still in the fast lane. To make matters worse, the road had been prepared for re-paving and the grooved surface made for a rough and noisy ride.

"I didn't have a radio or anything on. There was no one else in the car. All of a sudden, it was like this voice said, 'What are you doing? You've sensed this.' Immediately I realized I was ignoring the premonition and had actually increased my speed. I said to myself, 'This is silly not to listen to the warning.'" So she slowed down, signaled, and went into the middle lane.

"Then I heard this drop. On any ordinary day, with all the road noise, I would never have heard it. It was bizarre. Just this little noise." With that the rear wheel on the driver's side of her SUV flew off.

"I was going fast enough that when the wheel came off, the whole back end of the SUV dropped down and snapped the spare tire that was stored underneath. Now there were two tires flying off into rush hour traffic behind me. In my mirror I could see cars swerving trying to avoid these two tires that were bouncing through traffic. It was really a miracle that no one was hit." Her SUV started fishtailing out of control. At one point it went up and started to roll. She wrestled with the steering wheel and managed to get it back down. She still had three wheels but the condition of the road made it very challenging to control the vehicle. It was taking everything in her to fight it.

Tracy's situation was critical. She was nearly out of control in the middle lane in rush hour traffic between an exit ramp and a merge-on ramp.

"I remember I could see the cars going off behind me and the cars ahead of me coming on. I panicked. O my gosh, I thought. Someone's going to merge in and hit me and they don't know what's going on. I knew I was on the point of losing control of the vehicle. In that split second I cried out to God again: 'God, please help me. I don't want to die.'"

Up to this point, she had heard the cars skidding behind her. Now she couldn't hear anything. "There was absolute quiet in my vehicle. It was like time stood still. It was simply amazing. Then this warm light poured into my SUV and I was bathed in it. I want to say golden light—I don't know how to describe it. And there was this peace and this presence and this calm that came with it."

Then she heard a voice say, "There," and she remembers being focused beyond the top of the steering wheel, where her two hands were clamped onto it, to that specific spot where she felt she was being shown to go. "I don't know how I didn't get hit, because where I ended up stopping was at a merge-on ramp and the cars were just racing up to merge onto the thruway." The warm light remained with her all the while until she was safely at the shoulder of the road. Somehow she must have turned the motor off because she was just sitting there when somebody tapped on her window. It snapped her out of the daze she was in.

She got out and the gentleman standing there asked, "Are you all right?"

She said, "Yes, I'm okay."

He said, "I can't believe you walked away from that. You were thrown around like a rag doll in your truck."

Tracy had been wearing a seat belt and it wasn't until afterward that she realized she had some minor injuries.

Shaking his head, he said, "I can't believe nobody's hurt."

With that, she looked around. "I saw the cars spun out all over the highway. They were all stopped. When he said, 'Nobody's hurt,' I started to cry. It was unbelievable. There were no collisions. He actually brought my tires back to me. I can't believe one of those tires didn't hit and kill somebody. That was just God. There is no other explanation."

The man was wonderful—he phoned the police and stood with her until they came. After assessing the situation, the officer said, "No damage. No charges. We're not even going to write this up." Once the officer had gone, the man made sure she was all right and left.

Now Tracy felt uneasy—a young woman alone, stranded on the highway far from home—and she got back into the vehicle. At that point her brother phoned back. Right after the accident, Tracy had called him. He was coming to meet her.

"While I was talking with him, a strange man came and tapped on my window. I began to roll it down. I could hear my brother saying, 'Don't open your window. What are you doing? Somebody could hurt you.' This guy was kind of creepy. He really left me unsettled. For the first time I felt really vulnerable. With my brother on the phone I told the man, 'I've got somebody coming.' I rolled the window back up and locked the door." The man went away.

Sitting there in the SUV, she realized that one huge crisis had passed but now she faced two new dangers. It was starting to get dark. The tail-end of her SUV was sticking out into the merge-on lane. The cars were coming up the ramp so fast that Tracy was getting nervous that one of them might not see her SUV in the dark and would clip her and she'd be spun out into traffic. Yet if she gave up the safety of her locked vehicle, she'd be exposed to anyone lurking outside. She didn't know how much longer it would be before her brother would come. Finally, the danger of being hit overrode the other fear and she decided to get out of her vehicle. But not without a prayer to God: "I'm scared. Please protect me and be with me."

That's when a car came up with four young men in their early twenties. They got out and she explained what had happened. "At first I was nervous. I thought, Oh my gosh, I'm all alone and there's four of them. Your mind does strange things and you go to a dark place."

One of them said, "We're on our way to a Christian concert just down the highway. Would you like to come with us?"

She declined, saying that she was waiting for her brother to arrive. But inside a huge debate was going on. "Could I trust that they were sincere, God's people, real Christians? At the time I believed in God but I didn't know that He could be involved in my life or answer prayer like that. It was like reading about a book on the book jacket but not knowing what the story really is. I didn't have a real relationship with Him yet."

Even though she had said no, they stayed with her. "They stood with me for twenty to thirty minutes—just talking and sharing. They were really nice guys. Their presence calmed me and made me feel safe."

"Finally they said, 'Are you okay? We've got to go or we'll be late for the venue. If you get your car fixed, it's just down the road. We'd love to have you join us.'" They left.

Soon afterward, Tracy's brother arrived, followed shortly by the tow truck. Everything worked out and they were safely back in Windsor late that night.

After an accident like that, survivors often experience "post-traumatic stress" and Tracy had some of that. She also had post-traumatic change. The accident happened at what Tracy describes as "a horrendous time in our lives" for both her and her husband. The following spring, "things went from bad to worse" and by October their marriage had hit a wall. That was the turning point. Somehow she and her husband then began the journey of mending their marriage. God totally transformed and renewed their love and commitment to each other.

Looking back now, Tracy can see how her experience that day on the highway actually prepared her for the changes that were needed in her life. From childhood on, trust had been a huge issue for her. Her life was a whirlwind of effort to get everything right because she couldn't trust anyone else to do it as well as she could. But something had happened when God answered her prayers on the highway and spared her life. "He proved Himself to me," she says. "He introduced Himself as a trustworthy God." Proved, that is, that she, who struggled with trust, could trust Him. It took fully two years from the time of the accident for her finally to surrender and turn her life over to Christ. "It's Yours, not mine," she told Him.

"He started me on a journey of walking through my life in a new way. Previously, my lack of trust had taken the form of needing to control. It dominated my life. Now, in surrendering to Him, I released my control. I had been a perfectionist. God showed me that the message I had been sending my children and my husband was, 'There's only one way—my way!' No matter what they had done, my actions were saying it wasn't good enough. Now I saw that I wasn't being a blessing to them. My way is rarely the right way. The Lord has helped me to love my family by letting them be who they are, not what they had to be for me."

Tracy is the first to admit that she still hasn't got it all together. Today, after almost ten years of personal growth and change, she says, "It's an ongoing process of handing control over to God, moment by moment, situation by situation."

The wonder of that day on the highway has continued to reveal itself to her. Beyond the amazing deliverance of herself and her vehicle safely onto the roadside, and the safety of the other vehicles, Tracy has come to see a whole network of background blessings designed to keep her and others from harm—the man who brought the tires back, phoned the police, and stood by her, the timing of her brother's phone call, even the man who warned her about her tire beforehand.

Five or six years later Tracy was telling someone the part of the story about the four young men who drove up, when she stopped. "I realized that I had told God I was scared and asked for His protection, and He sent these four young men to stay with me, almost to the time my brother came. I had missed that blessing until then. He had provided! Actually, He answered many prayers that day. I wasn't alone. He put somebody there—even four of them. It was quite an experience that left a lasting imprint on my heart."

Angels On Kilimanjaro

Mount Kilimanjaro in Tanzania has been a source of intrigue and adventure ever since its summit was first reached in 1889 by Europeans Hans Meyer and Ludwig Purtscheller. Even earlier it had caught the popular imagination when it was first discovered by German missionaries in 1848. For years the world at large could not believe there could be snow and ice anywhere in central Africa. At 19,340 feet, it is Africa's tallest mountain. While not as high as Everest, which is part of a range, Kilimanjaro is the world's tallest free-standing mountain, rising 15,400 feet from its base. It has been described as "the shining mountain." Located only three degrees south of the equator, its summit is the farthest point on the earth's surface from the center of the earth.

For many different reasons it is a popular mountain for climbers, attracting about 25,000 a year. But it is a challenging mountain to climb—only fifteen percent reach the summit. And it is dangerous. Those who consider this mountain to be safe to climb are mistaken. At its heights the climber faces extremes of climate and swirling winds; at its lower reaches, carnivorous animals roam.

But the greatest challenge is the altitude. Even those in the very best condition are susceptible to high altitude pulmonary edema and high altitude cerebral edema when they do not take the time to let their bodies acclimatize to the increased altitude. Both conditions can be fatal. During the millennial celebrations on New Year's Day, when the mountain was thronged with over one thousand trekkers, three died and thirty-three more had to be rescued.

All of these challenges fired the imagination of Dr. Gordon Lawson, a fifty-three-year-old nutritionist, chiropractor, and complementary medicine specialist from Unionville, Ontario, Canada. He wanted to experience Africa. He wanted to raise money for prostate cancer research. But most of all, he wanted to overcome the challenge of the mountain, to push himself to new limits. All his life he had thrived on the thrill of adventure: walking the Columbia glaciers of Alberta, parasailing in the Caribbean, scuba diving on the Great Barrier Reef, car racing through the Alps. When he told me his Kilimanjaro experience, he had just returned from a trip with his wife to the Galapagos. While scuba diving at twenty meters, he encountered seven hammerhead sharks and enjoyed the view as they swam by. His passions still left to be achieved are to canoe the Nahanni Canyons in the Northwest Territories of Canada and to experience the rigors of Antarctica. Surprisingly, Kilimanjaro almost cost him his life.

The trip had been easy to arrange. Through a friend, he joined a group that was going. Other than gathering his gear and training, all he had to do was raise sponsorship money to support the cancer research project. So far as the training was concerned, he was already in excellent condition, routinely running forty kilometers a week. He stepped that up by climbing hills but neglected to go the added measure of training wearing a weighted backpack. It would be a generally easy path with some boulders and loose gravel. He told himself it would be just a matter of hiking. He was certain he would have no difficulty. He had researched pulmonary and cerebral edema but his attitude was "they affect other people, not me." So as he gathered the hiking boots, backpack, walking sticks, water bottles, and cold weather and rain gear, he had no concerns for either his health or safety.

But he had been so busy in his practice before leaving To-ronto that he was the last to arrive by air at Moshi in Tanzania. Moshi, at an elevation of about three thousand feet, is at the base of Kilimanjaro on the north side and marked the launch-ing pad for their trek to the summit. The other twenty-five members of the group had arrived earlier and had had time to rest and acclimatize themselves to the altitude. The next day their group was driven to the entrance of Kilimanjaro National Park and they began their trek. They climbed to about 12,000 feet and made camp. There were lovely open fields, cool but not cold. That first day they lost one camper who had to drop out. He had prostate cancer. His energy had been drained by getting to Moshi and he was having difficulty breathing.

They were told it was going down to freezing that night. Gordon shared a tent with Darren, another Canadian chiro-practor. Now he remembers that that first day he felt a slight soreness in his chest, a slight headache, and shortness of breath. But he ignored these symptoms and put them down to not enough training.

The next day they climbed to base camp at about 16,400 feet. There was no vegetation. It was all slag and desolate rocks and was quite cold. Gordon had to wear gloves and a toque. They arrived in the afternoon because they were going to do the assault on the summit the next day. Actually, they would begin the climb later that evening with the plan to arrive at the summit at 6:00 a.m. in time to see the sunrise. They were divided into two groups, the slow group leaving at 10:00 p.m. and the fast group leaving at 11:00 p.m. Gordon was in the fast group. The day, or more accurately the night, of the assault, Gordon continued to have symptoms of headache, sore throat, chest pain, and shortness of breath, but he told no one. He thought it was the strain of not training enough.

They were now climbing the steepest part of their journey and encountered "scree" on the rocky slope. Scree is a kind of gravel of pebbles and small stones which slides down as you walk on them, so that you sink with each step. It is heavy and exhausting walking. With each step Gordon became more fatigued. His shortness of breath increased and he experienced his heart racing. The mountain was taking its toll on others too. Six climbers had not proceeded from the base camp, and on this day of assault four more went back down. Gordon did not want to give up, and pushed on. They came to the summit of the old volcano, but it was not the highest point. As Gordon walked along the volcano rim he realized it would take another one and a half hours to reach the Uhuru Peak. He plodded on, past glaciers and cliffs. He heard the wonderful sound of the high wind blowing and felt the power and majesty of God. He was enchanted with the amazing sound of ice falling off the glacier and shattering into the crevasse below.

There was pathos and wonder in his voice as he told me, "That last one-and-a-half hour walk was unbearably slow because of the lack of oxygen. I took pictures looking out over the Indian Ocean. Marvelous! Then we started to come down."

He was becoming more and more fatigued. They had been warned about "the fatigue of the mountain." As he explained to me, "It takes three weeks to get to base camp at Everest. You have time to acclimatize. But at Kilimanjaro, the very next day I was climbing."

Going down was very slow. Even though going down the scree is very rapid—each step is two to three feet as you slide and sink—it is exhausting. Gordon couldn't keep up, even with Tom who was four years older.

Tom was the medical director for the group. Noticing Gordon's increasing difficulty, he kept asking Gordon, "Are you okay?"

Gordon answered routinely, "I'm fine. I'm just tired."

Tom said, "Wait for me. We'll go down together."

When Gordon got back to base camp, he drank some water and ate some food; but it was hardly down before he threw up.

One of the African guides said to him, "Man, you're very sick. You need to get down."

Gordon agreed. He was beginning to panic. When he got back to his tent, his tent buddy wasn't there. Sensing the urgency now, he grabbed his backpack and poles and left camp by himself. On his way out he told one of the African guides, "I'm going down."

He didn't wait for Tom. He knew he had to get down immediately.

Usually a climber feels better going down to where the oxygen is more plentiful. But Gordon, who had been experiencing shortness of breath, chest pain, headache, and fatigue, found the pain and fatigue increased as he descended. Two members of the group caught up with him and walked with him for a time, but he couldn't keep up. They carried his poles and backpack, but still he faltered. Then he had to put his arms around their shoulders for support. He was getting weaker as he went and could hardly shuffle his feet. Finally, he asked if they could just stop and rest for a minute. His heart was racing at 120 bpm. His normal resting rate was 48.

"As I sat there for a few minutes I realized I had pulmonary edema. I told the guys this and asked if they could find someone who could do something about it."

They were on the main trail and it wasn't long before a Swiss couple came by going up and then a Japanese man, also going up, but none of them could speak English. They went on. Then two couples came by, descending.

The people with Gordon called out, "Do you know anything about pulmonary edema?"

It turned out that one couple was from Germany but spoke English. The woman was a nurse and the man a cardiologist. She said, "Yes, we know something."

The cardiologist asked Gordon some questions. He had a stethoscope in his pocket and examined Gordon. "You've had this for quite a while, haven't you?" he asked.

Gordon replied, "Yes. I thought it was from carrying the backpack."

The cardiologist said, "This is very serious. You need three things: You need to take this puffer, you need to take this pill, and you need to take this injection."

Gordon remembers thinking in the distorted way an oxygen-deprived brain thinks, Why does this fellow want to push drugs on me? I don't like taking drugs. Out loud he said to the cardiologist, "I'm sure I'll be okay. Thank you very much. I just need to get down."

The cardiologist and his wife were dumbfounded. Exasperated, the German doctor threw up his hands. "So you don't need my treatment," he said angrily. "Then I believe you will be dead in fifteen to twenty minutes."

The critical danger he was in still did not register. In his growing stupor Gordon reflected to himself: What's in it for this fellow? What's his advantage to push drugs on me? Gordon couldn't think of a reason. Finally, with the shred of good sense he had remaining, he consented to the treatment.

As the injection went in he felt an incredible rush and fell back. The nurse caught him. Quite soon, some African guides came along and started to carry him down. They had gone only a short distance over a rise in the path when they were all amazed to see a gurney lying there by the trail—a makeshift stretcher with a wheel on the front. It was the one and only time on the entire trip that he saw anything resembling a stretcher. It was a godsend. As he said later, "If I had had to walk, I would not have made it to nightfall."

They placed him on the gurney and took him down to the base camp. There the cardiologist examined him that night and again the next morning and found him much improved. Gordon took a video of the doctor. It is to his great regret that later when he looked at the video, he could not make out either the doctor's name or address. He never saw him again. This man who was in Gordon's life for less than eighteen hours had saved his life.

When he returned home, medical examination showed a normal blood pressure and heart rate but revealed that indeed he had had a severe case of pulmonary edema. He had damaged the alveoli of his lungs and it would take six to eight weeks to make a full recovery.

He did exactly that and slowly returned to full strength. There were no scars or lasting effects. He was soon running his forty kilometers a week and keeping his hectic professional pace again.

In all too typical fashion the close call on Kilimanjaro hardly slowed him down. Instead it confirmed his expansive spirit. "I had a new sense of freedom. This experience showed me that God is in control of my coming and going. He still has something more for me to do."

His wife has no doubt whatever that God had rescued him. When Gordon was in crisis on the mountain, she had been sitting at her desk at home in Unionville doing paperwork when she had an overwhelming feeling that something was terribly wrong. The urgent thought came, "You have to pray." It was so acute that she didn't hesitate but knelt down with her face to the floor and prayed for more than twenty minutes for God to bless Gordon, whatever his situation might be. Only when she began to feel better did she stop praying and resume her work. After his return home, they calculated the time zone differences. They are certain that her time of prayer coincided with his time of greatest danger on the mountain and with the appearance of the cardiologist and his wife. She also noted that even before Gordon had left for the trip, her family, which is Catholic, had arranged for novenas to be offered on his behalf.

Then There Was One

Statistics are always baffled by the exceptional individual. Certainly, statistics have their place in analyzing trends, in organizing diverse events and groups of people into predictable categories and numbering them off according to probabilities. But they do not know how to deal with the one person who lies outside the lines. In fact they are concerned with the potential and the abstract, not the actual and the real. Statistics talk about "what if," while the exceptional individual reveals "what is." What a person is cannot be smoothed out to a norm and, as we all know, individuals are unpredictable.

The events of Russell's life make him one of a kind, beyond all prediction or classification. His is a remarkable story of one escape after another. He has survived so many accidents that his wife of fifty-eight years just shakes her head and tells him, "God is not ready for you to come home yet." When I sat down with him to get the details of an amazing escape from death, four other stories tumbled out of him as well.

Let's begin when Russell was still in his twenties. It was July 1959. As marketing sales manager for a major Canadian electronics firm, Russell had flown to Montreal with five of his salesmen for a five-day conference. As they finished the final session Friday afternoon and were coming out of the building to catch the six o'clock flight home, his boss called Russell back. He had some specifications on a new TV camera tube he needed to go over with Russell. It would only take five to ten minutes, the boss assured him. The five salesmen went ahead without him. They left at 4:45. After the brief meeting, Russell called a cab to go to the airport by himself. It was 5:15 when he left.

Normally the trip took twenty minutes. There would be lots of time, he assured himself. On the way to the airport, however, the traffic was more congested than usual, even for rush hour. A few minutes into the drive, he knew it would be close.

The driver shared his own concern: "I don't understand it. I've been driving cabs for twenty years, and I've never seen it like this." As they crept along and the minutes ticked away, he shook his head: "I'm afraid we're not going to make the airport on time."

"There's an extra twenty in it if you do," said Russell.

"I don't care if it's a hundred. We're not going to make it," came the abrupt reply.

Sitting there, helpless in the back of the cab, Russell was angry and frustrated that the boss had left it so close. "If it had been me, we would have been out of there by four thirty. But he was the boss."

The driver took side streets, back roads, alleys, every short-cut he knew, trying to make up time. No use. They arrived at the airport at one minute past six.

Russell recalls, "I ran to the check-in. The gate was closed. The flight was on the runway awaiting takeoff."

He resigned himself to the fact and booked the next flight at seven.

Russell continued, "Then I went down to the lounge for a sandwich and coffee. The news was on TV. As I watched, an announcer interrupted the broadcast to say that Flight 83,

Silver Dart Service Montreal to Toronto, had crashed. There were no survivors. There was a terrible thunderstorm, pitch black, you couldn't see anything. I ran back to the check-in to see if all five men had made the flight. All five were on it." Russell was stunned.

"I phoned my wife to tell her and couldn't get through for half an hour. She went through agony. She thought I'd been on that flight."

He should have been. "That's what my ticket was for. If the manager hadn't stopped me, I would have been on that flight."

It didn't really sink in until Monday morning. That's when Russell realized, "There're five men who are not going home to their families." They averaged about thirty years of age. He was twenty-eight and he and his wife had four children under five. He knew he was very fortunate. At the time he was a nominal churchgoer and didn't see it in terms of God. "I flew so often, I just accepted it as one of those breaks." But an impression was being made.

Less than ten years later, in 1967, he was driving his brand new Ford custom on a dry three-lane highway in daylight when suddenly a van was sideways directly in front of him, blocking two lanes. Shifting abruptly to the right to go around the van, he was rear-ended by a loaded transport truck. When everything came to a stop, the truck had pushed right up to the back of the front seat of Russell's car. "I could touch his chrome bumper with my hand," Russell gestures. "The whole back of my car was missing. I should have been crushed, but I walked away without a scratch." The car was a write-off.

Most of his miraculous escapes involved aircraft and flying. In his job, he would log over 100,000 air miles a year. One of these close calls was a mid-air near-collision over O'Hare Field in Chicago. It was the early seventies. The stretch DC8 with 298 passengers and crew was approaching O'Hare Field. It had descended from 43,000 feet and was on its final approach for landing when, without warning, another DC8 was coming directly at them from the side. They were so close he could see the terrified look on the faces of the pilot and co-pilot. It seemed like a certain collision, with the lives of over six hundred people at stake. Immediately he heard the wheels being retracted under them and saw the other plane dive, passing beneath them with what seemed like only inches to spare. Everyone landed safely with no injuries.

Two years later, he was one of three passengers on a small Cessna aircraft. As the plane touched down to land, the nose wheel assembly collapsed, forcing the other two wheels to give way as the weight of the plane came onto them. The pilot was faced with a most difficult choice. Applying the brakes would almost certainly cause the plane to nose into the runway, flip over, and likely explode; so he had to let the plane grind its way down the runway on its belly and hope there would be enough distance to let friction bring the plane to a safe stop. By the time they came to rest, all of the undercarriage was worn off. Amazingly, all four occupants, including Russell, emerged without a scratch.

Each of these occurred in the course of routine travel. The last dramatic escape happened during a test flight of sorts. In the late 1970s, in his role as sales manager, he was investigating a complaint that the bearings on the rotor shaft of helicopters used by the Canadian Air Force were failing. Two people had died in fatal crashes. His company's bearings were suspect. He decided to see for himself and arranged for a test flight in one of the helicopters. As he and the pilot approached the helicopter, he asked why it was parked on the grass rather than the tarmac as it usually was. The pilot did not know. Getting in, he instructed the pilot to go straight up so that he could see the effect of the full pressure on the bearings. He watched the temperature in the bearing housing. As it came to the critical 900 degree C level, the rotor shaft seized and the helicopter plummeted straight down more than fifty feet and buried the helicopter up to its doors in the earth. He and the pilot, while shaken, walked away unhurt. It was then he realized how fortunate it was that the helicopter had been parked on grass and not tarmac!

Afterward, he confronted those responsible for maintenance of the helicopter. "Those were not our bearings," he asserted. "I know for certain, because they failed at 900 degrees C and ours are good to 1200." Those in charge admitted they had used competitor's bearings to save money, and that's what had caused the crashes.

Reflecting on his long life and these many escapes, Russell now sees the hand of God in a more personal way. "He's certainly sparing me for many things right up to the present." He doesn't understand the tragedy of those who died in the air crash, nor why he should have been saved. But for him there is no doubt that Someone intervened to keep him off that fatal flight.

Faith Walk To Rescue A Princess

Bert and Terry were sitting with their wives by Bert's RV at a campground near Port Canaveral, Florida. They had been friends for years and were enjoying the relaxed banter as evening darkened around them. Suddenly, Bert sat forward in his chair and said, "I think I'll go for a walk."

"I'll come with you," said Terry, and the two men got to their feet.

Looking back at his wife, Bert said, "I need the flashlight."

She protested that there was plenty of light. She was right. All around them the roads and parks of the trailer park were well lit.

Bert insisted. "Get the flashlight, please." She brought it to him, and the men went off on their walk.

Bert had an inner certainty about what he was doing. In his personal walk with the Lord he had learned to obey the prompting of the Spirit. He hadn't heard anything as definite as words, but sitting there in the twilight he knew that he must go on this walk, right then. There was something vitally important for him to do.

Terry was skeptical when it came to matters of faith. He had known Bert long enough to respect these hunches, even though they were beyond his comprehension. He just went along as company for Bert.

At first they followed a main roadway where the light was good. Beyond the campground limits, however, they were soon surrounded by darkness. When the road bent to the left Terry began to go that way, but Bert said, "No, this way," indicating a dirt path to the right in the deep shadows. As they followed it around some bushes, the beam of the flashlight revealed used hypodermic needles, broken beer bottles, and trash on the ground. Terry, who was a policeman back home, hesitated. "This is not a good place to be," he whispered in the darkness.

Bert didn't stop. He was on a mission. They followed the path further, the beam of the flashlight now their only guide in the total darkness. At last, winding through a thicket of tangled bushes, they found themselves on a beach. Over the sound of waves gently lapping the shore, they could hear a faint whimpering. As Bert extended the beam further, it revealed a little girl in a frilly party costume, huddled there on the coarse sand. Not wanting to frighten her by coming too close, Bert said, "We're here to help you. What is your name and what are you doing here?"

"My name is Rosalee★. I'm trying to find my mother."

Hearing those words and seeing this innocent, lost child melted their hearts. Within him, Bert sensed the Spirit caution them not to touch her but to guide her at a safe distance—wise guidance to prevent any later suspicions about their motives.

"I'll shine the flashlight on the path ahead of you," Bert told her. "Follow the light and we'll take you to your mother."

Something told him to go back by the same path. The return journey was much slower, however, considering the pace at which she could walk and them needing to reassure her often. When they arrived at last at the outskirts of the trailer park they could hear faint shouts in the distance. As they went further, the shouts grew louder. "Rosalee. Rosalee!" It was her parents and family members who had been searching for her. They were frantic. When at last they came into view, Rosalee bolted for her mother and was caught up in her arms and smothered with kisses.

Seeing that she was unharmed, they were immensely relieved. Rosalee was only about seven years old and had been missing for hours. Her parents, haunted by imaginary images, had feared the worst. Now in the excitement of her safe return, the parents and family didn't notice as Bert and Terry faded from the scene.

On the way back to the RV Terry turned to Bert. "How did you know?"

"It's the Lord," said Bert simply. "He's so good when we listen to Him."

Terry just scratched his head.

A skeptic might counter that Bert has a natural gift of intuition. He was just picking up the psychic vibrations from an unknown dimension of awareness. Yes, he was receiving a communication of some kind, but it wasn't natural. The question turns on what Bert heard and who Bert is. He had a conversion experience forty years ago and his whole life since has been lived in a faith relationship with Jesus Christ. His business life, his finances, his family life, and his community service are all filled with examples of how God guides and works through him. He's a Gideon working to distribute Scriptures locally and internationally. Sunday by Sunday he worships at the Salvation Army, where he's on the Board. No one knows the number of people he has helped come to faith in Christ. This spiritual nudge is just one instance of the Lord's activity in his life.

When he got back to the RV, he leaned back in his favorite lawn chair, relaxed, and thanked the Lord for letting them find Rosalee.

SUFFERING

From a secular perspective suffering would seem to be the last place God would come. It is a popular assumption that people who suffer have been abandoned by God or are being punished by God. Certainly, it's reasonable to think that people who have suffered hardships in life would be angry and resentful that God had not spared them or rescued them from pain and difficulty. Yet the opposite is often true. It is the person who has been brought low with hardship who often is most ready to be dependent on God's mercy. Many have found God in the midst of suffering who had never known Him in good times.

The central symbol of Christianity is the cross, which at the very least locates suffering in the heart of God. That explains as well how Christians find great spiritual benefit in suffering borne gladly with faith. The Apostle James says, "Count it all joy when you fall into various trials, knowing that the testing of your faith produces patience. But let patience have its perfect work, that you may be perfect and complete, lacking nothing" (James 1:2–4 NKJV).

His Wonderful Face

On March 31, 1988, Chris Landry and his wife, Margot, were preparing to make the forty-five-minute trip from their home in rural Ontario to pick up Chris's daughter at Lester B. Pearson International Airport in Toronto. As they were leaving, he dumped the remaining tea from his cup into the sink. That was the last thing he remembered for a long time.

He was the driver as they proceeded south on the country road in their Honda Acura around seven p.m. It was dark, but the road was clear and dry. No cars were in front of them, but two vans were driving toward them, their lights on. Suddenly, at a slight crest and dip in the road, the second van pulled out to pass, hitting Chris head-on. At the last minute, Chris tried to avoid the impact by steering to the right onto the shoulder, but the van hit the Honda on the left front bumper and drove the motor, wheel, and steering assemblies back into Chris's helpless body.

Nine weeks later he regained consciousness to learn that he had been involved in a near-fatal accident. Margot had sustained several fractures but was in fairly good condition. However, he had been very seriously hurt. His left hip, which had sustained the major impact, had multiple fractures. His thighbone had been driven back, badly smashing his left hip. His pelvis was completely split. Of greatest concern to the doctors, because of the amount of bleeding and internal damage, was the possibility of a fatal stroke. Altogether he received seventeen units of blood, one of which contained the Hepatitis C virus, as he was to find out seven years later.

Lying there in his room after weeks in the intensive care unit, the first thing he was aware of was the four metal spikes, eighteen inches long, that pierced and protruded from his pelvis on either side of his abdomen. They were connected by metal bridgework which held him together and would gradually be pushed closer together as the pelvis healed overtime. His left leg was straight out in traction for many weeks. Chris was a big man, 6' 2" and 280 pounds at the time of the accident. When he was finally released from the hospital seventeen weeks later he weighed 198 pounds.

For sixteen of the seventeen weeks, he had those spikes in him. Where the metal and the skin met were open sores. Several times a day the dressings on those sores had to be changed—a painful process. That was where Chris received unexpected help.

At the time Chris called himself a "lapsed churchman." He remembered, though, the ceramic plaque of the face of Jesus that had hung over the doorway to his bedroom when he was a kid. "When they came to change the dressings, His face would be what I'd see." The words of a hymn came too:

> "Turn your eyes upon Jesus,
>   Look full in His wonderful face,
>   And the things of earth will grow strangely dim,
>   In the light of His glory and grace."[9]

As they changed the dressings, Chris would say those words over and over to himself. "I could see the pain in His face, and that would take my pain away. I mean, it was gone! I had no recurrence of the pain again until the next time they would change

---

9. Text by Helen H. Lemmel.

the dressings." To this day, Chris has no doubt that Jesus was there with him in those times of pain and that is why he had no panic that the pain would be too much. Every day in the hospital he would read his Bible and found strength there too.

Margot would visit, being sure to take her own neck brace off before coming in so as not to worry him. What she could not hide, however, was the reality of their financial situation. Bills were piling up, and Chris, who was self-employed, was without any income or benefits.

He had had an outstanding twenty-year career, rising through various marketing and sales positions. He had been president and general manager of a major automotive chemicals company for three years before launching out as a consultant on his own. The accident came, though, at a time when their finances were vulnerable, and Chris did not know what he could do about it. He prayed for God's help.

Out of the blue a phone call came from the president of one of the companies Chris consulted for.

"How's it going?" the man asked.

"Terrible! Margot was just in and we're out of money."

"Send me a bill," the president said matter-of-factly.

"What do you mean?" Chris asked. "I can't do anything."

"You can answer the phone, can't you?" countered the executive. "It will be worth it to just get your input." The first check was for $5,000.00.

"That kind of divine provision has continued to this day," Chris affirms. "I take it to God, and He looks after it."

The story of God's interventions could stop there with Chris's survival, the spiritual transformation of his pain by the visions of Jesus' face, and the generosity of his executive friend. But these were only the most dramatic and obvious signs of God's activity, and only the beginning. More subtle was the way in which Chris was sustained through the huge medical and surgical challenges that followed. In the sixteen years from 1992 to 2007 he had a total of six hip replacements, was diagnosed with Hepatitis C, had persistent bone infections for two years, and received multiple courses of chemotherapy for his Hepatitis C. Yet, amazingly, Chris was able to see all of this in a positive light.

"God wanted to change my life walk. And He did. He didn't want to end it."

Why is still the exciting part of it for Chris. He keeps finding new ways in which he is being changed by the accident.

"There is no real comparison between before and now. Before, I was self-focused, cocky, not very spiritual. Now I look outward to others, how to use my gifts, and I'm more aware of being loving to others. I'm not as facile or flippant. I'm a better listener, more empathic, more conscious of where I fail. I'd like to think I've traded excess for gentleness. It's a very strange process."

Also, he's finding new opportunities because of his own sufferings. After his initial recovery, Chris was asked to work with a young man who was confined to a wheelchair with multiple sclerosis and to engage him in some activity as therapy. Previously Chris had no time for death and disease. He shrank from the thought of touching the skin of a sick person. But that's what he was being asked to do—the very thing others had done for him.

"God wanted me to learn that for me to touch other people's skin was no different than my skin. I literally had to pick him up and I didn't want to—but I did. A valuable lesson!"

For three months he daily spent time with a friend who was dying and supported him through his final days, something he would never have been able to do before. As far as gentleness is concerned, high on his priority list is going to his local library on Saturday mornings and reading to the children.

About five years ago Chris began training as a lay preacher in his local Protestant church. That too has been a walk of personal growth and discovery.

"When I first preached, I would spend hours writing out the notes. Then one day I heard God saying, 'Put down your notes.' After that, I would go through the whole week without writing, just being intimate with God, listening. In communication, Him holding me up, preparing me for what He wanted me to say."

Although he doesn't preach much any more, Chris says, "In my prayers, He's still there."

I asked him about anger.

"No. I wasn't angry with the other driver, or with God. But I was angry with the situation, that I was helpless, like a baby. I had to work on that. That's what led to a new life."

The divine element in Chris's story is seen in the positives that come through in spite of hardship and suffering. In the early days in the hospital, the traction and the ache in his leg associated with it were almost unbearable at times, but the handle on the pulley gave him some ability to move his leg and relieve it. Also, the patients he saw around him were revelations to him.

"God showed me others who were far worse off than I was, so that by comparison my condition was nothing." He saw patients who simply rose above their handicap by the power of a spirit that would not be defeated.

"I saw paraplegics in wheelchairs doing wheelies. People just adjust to things."

What has he learned about God from all this?

"That He can use you; there is always a bigger and better plan. With God it's a dynamic process with multiple opportunities. Not something fixed or closed—but a purpose and a plan that is still developing. That's exciting. Love is dynamic, and I believe I'm loved."

Freedom From Self

God is a contrarian. Those who are humbled by life and know their insufficiency receive from God's abundance. Those who are confident in themselves and think they are sufficient are left with their insufficiency. It is the ones whose lives are bent and broken who so often come to know God, while those who are stuck with their egos are on the outside looking in. "The Son of Man came to seek and to save the lost" (Luke 19:10 NIV).

Matt★ has had more than his share of losses. He is one of the deprived who never knew affection as a child and grew up lonely, with all the emptiness and self-doubt that come with such experiences. The painful vacuum inside meant that he would try to draw life from others to fill his own and never be satisfied. That was to be the pattern in his marriage.

Matters got much worse with the crib death of their second child. It was then that Matt crossed the line into alcohol abuse to fill the deepening void within him. Instead he found that it left him emptier than before.

On every side he began encountering the deficits of his life. He never got the education that his intelligence deserved. His emotional wounds made it difficult to develop a career or hold a job for long. He was limited to low-paid, seasonal employment.

Finally, when his wife left after twenty-three years of marriage, Matt was devastated.

"I lost what was nearest and dearest to me—my control. I couldn't find words for the pain I was in. I cried every day for seven months. I prayed, 'Bring her back. Tell me if she's coming back.'"

The answer was "No."

By some amazing coincidence, six days after his wife left, on Epiphany, January 6, 1992, Matt stopped drinking and has been a recovering alcoholic ever since. At sixty, divorced, living alone, father of two, alienated from one who has not spoken to him in twenty years, Matt has known more than his share of trouble.

What about the flip side of the equation? Today Matt is a man who passionately loves God. He knows his Bible from the inside out. He has proven in action the truths it contains. For him, faith is not a theory but a practical necessity every day. His purpose now is to help others who struggle with addiction. His best hours are given to others. For all his suffering, Matt could fill a book with stories of how God has become real in his life. Here are just three.

Eight years ago Matt was at a particularly low point. For several days he lay in bed with back pain. He lived alone in his house in a farming community with no one to care for him. He couldn't work or even get up because of the pain in his back. Finally, lying there, he cried out in desperation, "Lord, take this pain away."

A storm had been gathering slowly outside. Within moments of his prayer there was a lightning strike so close by the house that everything within the house was charged with electricity. The answering machine jumped and spouted alarm noises. Matt was lifted inches off the bed he was lying on. When he collected his senses and realized he was unharmed, only dazed, he sat up on the bed. It was then he discovered the pain was gone. What is more, it never returned.

Now he says, "Up to that time I had never prayed for any physical healing. Since then, I even pray about a hangnail." Desperate circumstances inspire huge leaps of faith.

Matt has found that many of his experiences have been so unusual and miraculous that they could just as well have come right out of Scripture. In fact, some of them have involved passages in the Bible. Five years ago a strange coincidence occurred while he was reading a passage from Ecclesiastes. The context is vital to appreciate what happened. At the time the porch on his house was in a terrible state of disrepair. He was unemployed and could not afford to fix it. The rafters sagged, insulation hung down in clumps, and the roof leaked when it rained. With the struggles of his life, being divorced, a recovering alcoholic, and alienated from his children, he lacked motivation to do anything about it. It was all he could do to stay on the Alcoholics Anonymous program with God's help.

That day he happened to be reading some verses from Ecclesiastes before going to an A.A. meeting when the silence was broken by a loud crash outside the door. Going out, he discovered that part of the roof had fallen in on the porch. Resigned to the misfortune, he went to the meeting. When he returned and sat down again to the Bible lying open on the table, the first verse he read on the open page was Ecclesiastes 10:18: "Through laziness, the rafters sag; because of idle hands, the house leaks" (NIV).

God had spoken in such an obvious way that Matt was ashamed. "I was heartbroken that I needed chastising like that. I was being reprimanded for being lazy, just like a little kid. That night I got down on my knees and asked God to forgive me. When I got up off my knees, there on the Billy Graham wall calendar I saw the verse for that day: 'If we confess our sins, he is faithful and just to forgive us our sins, and to cleanse us from all unrighteousness'" (1 John 1:9 KJV). He was discovering how God's mercy shines through His judgment.

Finding God's will for his life has been Matt's repeated prayer focus for the last five years. Just recently, he came home, flicked through some TV channels, and finally left it on a religious channel he hardly ever watched. It soon faded into the background. Going across the room, he opened his Bible at random and read three or four verses that caught his eye: "Rejoice evermore. Pray without ceasing. In every thing give thanks: for this is the will of

God in Christ Jesus concerning you" (1 Thessalonians 5:16–18 KJV). He stopped to think of his old question of God's will for him. Then he went on to read the rest of the chapter. As he was reading from verse 20 on, he could hear the man on TV reading the exact same words he was reading, word for word: "Prove all things; hold fast that which is good. Abstain from all appearance of evil. And the very God of peace sanctify you wholly; and I pray God your whole spirit and soul and body be preserved blameless unto the coming of our Lord Jesus Christ. Faithful is he that calleth you, who also will do it" (21–24).

Matt asked, "What are the chances of that? Prohibitive! I immediately realized the fantastic: There He goes again! Nothing He does surprises me anymore. He's saying, 'Matt, I'm with you always. I love you. I'm looking after you. I care about you to such an extent that I'll give you this incredible experience. I can show you what immense power I have that I can engineer things like this, and how immensely I love you.'"

That would be wonder enough. But the amazing coincidence opened to an even deeper awareness. The words he had read contained the answer to his prayer about God's purpose for him: "In every thing give thanks: for this is the will of God in Christ Jesus concerning you" (1 Thessalonians 5:18 KJV). He realized God was asking him not to do some special mission, but simply to be thankful in his situation. At the time Matt was being tested severely by rejection from others. For most of his life it had been overly important for him to be liked. Now he was getting the message to seek to please only God and to let other self-concerns go.

Matt is a textbook example of a man whose suffering has brought him first-hand knowledge of God's power and love. Perhaps the greatest lesson he has learned is the freedom of self-surrender. As he explained to me, our own efforts to solve our basic life problems are doomed to fail because when they fail they fail, and when they succeed they further imprison us in pride, self-salvation, and the illusion of self-control. He quotes the words of Archbishop William Temple: "No effort of the self can remove the self from the center of its own endeavor."[10] Suffering showed him that he could not save himself. Trusting himself to God set him free of himself.

The Fall ... Of Disbelief

It was fall—a time of truth when trees give up the boasts and extravagances of summer foliage for the naked honesty of November. It was fall—a time of reckoning when nature takes its essentials into storage for the winter. It was fall—reminding me how we come to our essential selves in death. Memories of Ted Kennedy's funeral were still fresh—those words of his plaintive appeal to the Pope for mercy being read in the descending twilight of Arlington Cemetery. However liberal in the summer of life, we tend to become more conservative as we sift life to its final resting place. It was fall—and my friend Jimmie was dying.

---

10. William Temple, *Nature, Man and God* (Edinburgh: R & R Clark, 1934).

He had been diagnosed with advanced cancer of the esoph-
agus. When I visited him in the hospital, the shock of the diagnosis was still on him. "I'm going to have to make some major
revisions in my thinking," he said quietly. Legal details and funeral
plans were no doubt on his mind. The doctors could do nothing
medically for him and he was sent home.

Jimmie was a veteran Canadian actor with a long and distinguished career in theater, film, and television in Canada, the United States, and Britain. He and his wife had lived for many years
in the village. Jimmie was a strong and colorful personality who
polarized people. He could be as witty and charming as an elf and
as cantankerous as a pit bull. Fortunately, his wife, Myfanwy, was
a peacemaker and caregiver. Both were community-minded and
the village loved them.

They lived in a quaint house next to the village church. He
came to worship from time to time but did not have a happy
relationship with some members of the congregation. They, being Baptist, did not understand his unorthodox spirituality or appreciate his outspoken criticism of their strict biblical positions.
He considered their evangelical, Jesus-centered faith too narrow
and restrictive. On more than one occasion he had walked out
of church in the middle of the sermon in protest over what was
being said.

Some members of the congregation befriended him and
supported him in his valiant efforts to extend his career in semi-
retirement. Those who were patient enough to listen might piece
together the roots of his discontent. He had an artist's tempera-
ment and a crusader's sensitivity to the needs of the outcast, so

that he put people before principle and tolerance before creed. Since early childhood his religious development had been guided by an aunt who exposed him to a broad spectrum of spirituality and a liberal belief system. His dramatic craft gave him a natural yearning for liturgical worship. It was no secret that he much preferred the Anglican prayer-book service to the Spartan plainness of Baptist worship. The esoteric fringes of theology attracted him and he had assembled an extensive library on mystical approaches to the Bible and Christianity. When he fell ill, sometime before the cancer diagnosis, the congregation put him on their prayer list for healing and for salvation.

It was fall and Jimmie did not have a certain faith as he faced an uncertain future. Over the six years of our friendship, we had spoken of many things—of plays and playwriting, of musicals and plot advancement, of Shakespeare and Stephen Leacock, of the uses of conflict, irony, pathos, and humor, of finances in the theater and the politics of producers. But now we spoke of God. He made it plain to me, as his friend, that he could not share the faith we at the church had about salvation in Jesus. To him it was far broader and more inclusive than that. "You folks at the church sound so sure about Jesus. I could never believe in Him in such a simplistic and personal way." Still he allowed me to read scripture and to pray with him. Afterward he asked if I would send him a copy of the biblical passages I had read that day.

Life has a way of bunching things up. Although their house had been for sale for almost a year, it was at this stressful time that it finally sold. Both village and church honored them with farewells and they moved to be near the acting community that he loved so much.

It happened that a former minister of the village church lived close to the city to which they moved. He and Jimmie had a good relationship and Jimmie asked him if he would help him plan his funeral service. It was comforting for many at the church to know that that person would be ministering to him during his last days. Not long afterward, Myfanwy asked if I would send a book Jimmie had given me when he had been dispersing his library. It contained readings from an alternative Gnostic gospel that he wanted to include in his funeral service. I did so.

Six weeks later I discovered he had been taken to the hospital in very poor condition, and I visited him there. He told me that two days previously he was certain he was going to die and had pleaded to be taken to the hospital. There he had rallied after they gave him a blood transfusion and he was doing quite well. So well, in fact, that now he was determined to go home again. He felt imprisoned in that hospital room. But, as he said, by asking to be taken to the hospital he had "dug himself a hole" and only had himself to blame. Now he couldn't leave without cutting off his chance of returning when he was desperate again. I listened quietly but could do nothing to solve his problem. After a brief prayer, I left.

Two days later, on Saturday afternoon, my phone rang around 5:30 p.m. It was Jimmie and he had exciting news. "The doctor came in this afternoon at the end of her rounds. She decided to grant my wish and send me home. She ordered a hospital bed for me at home so that I could be as comfortable as possible. It's amazing how quickly they got it all done. The deadline for the bed was four o'clock and they got it before that. I'm at home now in bed and feeling such relief. It will be much easier for Myfanwy to manage with the bed. They will be sending nurses every day to get me up in the morning and to settle me in for the night. The doctor warned me that it would get much worse. But I'm happy to be home where I can die in peace."

Then he added something I could hardly believe. "George, the other thing I want to tell you is that I've had an epiphany. It's as if the mist has parted and I can see clearly now. I want to change my funeral readings. I want Christ to be at the center of my funeral."

Tears filled my eyes and I was silent for a long moment. I didn't want to presume too much and I wasn't quite certain that I had heard correctly. Stalling until I could be sure what he meant, I said, "Tell me when you feel comfortable about letting the church people know."

"You can tell them tomorrow," was his immediate response.

"What would you want me to say?" I asked.

"Tell them that I am trusting my life to Jesus."

Next morning during the announcement period at church I reported Jimmie's statement of faith in Jesus to the congregation. Afterward, in the coffee hour, the head of the prayer team came to me. He was a long-time resident of the village and an old friend of Jimmie and Myfanwy. After thanking me for what I had shared about Jimmie, he told me that earlier that very morning before church he had received a phone call from his own youngest daughter, Karen.

She had told him, "Dad, in the night I had the strangest dream of Jimmie Douglas. I don't know what to make of it. In the dream he is standing in front of me outside the church. It is a blue-sky day. It feels like fall. Jimmie is desperate to get into the church but cannot. He's nicely dressed—a fine wool check blazer with patches on the elbows, brown dockers, and on his feet a pair of laced up loafers—but the loafers are covered with debris—pine needles and leaves. I go to him and brush off all the debris and wipe his shoes clean with my hand. When I finished I led him up the steps to the landing in front of the church door. It was a heavy door and I wondered how he was going to open it, yet as he reached out it seemed to open itself. There was no expression on his face, but I had the sense of peace over him. He went in and the door closed after him."

He told me that his daughter had known Jimmie since she was a girl. The man said, "Now I understand what her dream is about."

Almost two weeks passed before I spoke with Jimmie again on the phone. Someone had reported the dream to him. "It's wonderful, isn't it?" Jimmie exclaimed. "I've gone up the steps and I've entered that sanctuary. I have a sense of peace."

I was relieved to hear his positive response because frankly I wondered if his initial enthusiasm might have faded. I asked him to tell me more of what had happened to give him his new faith. "For the first time Jesus is a very real person. He is Someone you can talk to as a friend when you're in trouble." It was clear that he had had a personal encounter with Jesus, that it was an ongoing relationship for him and a source of great comfort and enthusiasm.

Jimmie's daughter and stepchildren had been regular visitors over the months of his illness. Now, just before Christmas, his two sons traveled long distances for an extended visit with him. For five days they had a rollicking good time. They put together a graphic of Jimmie as a dancing elf and sent it out as an email to his whole network of family and friends. "We've been hearing from people from all over the world," his wife said. "It's been wonderful for Jimmie."

These visits were just coming to an end on December 20 when I checked in by phone to see how he was progressing. "My faith is still very strong. Jesus the Christ is still very real to me."

"What has changed?" I asked.

"There's a tremendous strength I didn't have before. I am surrounded by so much love. It boils down to an absolute simplicity of faith." Then with a mischievous note he added, "The more I articulate this faith to people the more it rebounds in them. I can hear scales of disbelief clanging to the floor." Like a good actor he left some suspense about his meaning.

There was no ambiguity, though, about where his own hope lay now for the future. "I am a man who has searched all my life for my own personal truth and have now found it."

On December 28, I phoned Jimmie to say I had a cold and would not be able to visit as I had hoped. He assured me again about his faith. I asked him what he believed lay ahead for him. "Opposite my bed is a wall I see all the time. There's a piece of furniture and a frame with a narrow gap between them. I keep looking into the gap and what I see is Jesus the Christ coming toward me with His arms reaching out."

"And His face?" I asked.

"The look on His face is absolute serenity."

My friend Jimmie was dying, but now he was ready. He asked me to bless him. I gave him the promise of Jesus in John 14: "I go to prepare a place for you. And if I go and prepare a place for you, I will come again and receive you to Myself; that where I am, there you may be also. And where I go you know, and the way you know" (2b–4 NKJV).

Like the gentleman he was, his last words to me were "Thank you, George."

Jimmie died peacefully the next day at home with his dear wife by his side.

An interesting postscript was added the following day. I was speaking with Karen's mother about the dream Karen had of Jimmie trying to get up the steps into church and of her cleaning pine needles from his shoes. We agreed the timing was remarkable coming as it did the night after he had told me of his new faith, the night before I would announce it in the church. "But have you heard the most amazing thing?" she went on. "Myfanwy told me that that same night Jimmie had a vision in which he saw Christ walking in a pine forest."

A pine forest? you may ask. Being an evergreen, the pine tree is well known as a symbol of eternal life.

THE POWER OF THE RESPONSE

In fact, the power is in the response. Viktor Frankl, the renowned psychiatrist and founder of logotherapy, has said that the one thing no one can take away from you is your freedom to choose how you will respond to whatever others do to you.[11] He should know. A prisoner for several years in Nazi work camps during World War II, in desperately unhealthy conditions, and forced to work, often to the point of exhaustion, Frankl maintained that it was a sense of purpose that kept him going. Knowing that he had a meaning to live out gave him an attitude toward the rigors of prison life that refused to give up. In the face of the most trying circumstances, he responded with determination and hope.

Sometimes we find ourselves making excuses and blaming others. "You make me mad!" we may blurt out in an argument. But the truth is we choose to be angry. Equally, it is our freedom to choose not to be angry.

In the stories that follow, individuals, bowed down with great trials and with understandable reason to cast aside to despair or worse, chose instead to make something worthwhile out of what life had left them.

---

11. Viktor E. Frankl, *Man's Search for Meaning* (Boston: Beacon, 2002).

Six Hundred Haitians

Our small Bible study group was discussing how God brings blessings out of tragedies. Near the close, Earl, who uses a cane because of a recent stroke, said in passing, "Then there's the case of my son who was killed in a car crash twenty-two years ago and my grandson who was with him who has been an invalid ever since." Others in the group who knew the story nodded, and the meeting closed soon after without any further explanation.

Afterward my wife and I walked slowly down the hall with Earl, in pace with his severe limp. Despite the partial paralysis of his whole left side, Earl wears a firm smile on his face with a twinkle in his eye. I took the opportunity to ask him for more details. He confirmed that his twenty-seven-year-old son had been killed in a head-on crash years before and that his young grandson has been on life-support ever since.

"What blessing could possibly come out of such tragic losses?" I asked.

"Well," he replied as he bobbed steadily up and down using the cane, "for one thing, it changed my life. For another, there're those six hundred Haitians."

Now we were standing by the elevator. Before he got on, he agreed to tell me the full story later.

It was Earl's seventy-sixth birthday a few days later when we sat down under a tree on his patio in Holmes Beach, Florida.

"My wife and I have been living here for fifty-five years," he began. "We came from Canton, Ohio."

Soon after they arrived he had established a TV sales and service business there on Anna Maria Island off of Bradenton. With hard work and dependability the business took off.

"We had three sons, fifteen months apart," he told me. "As they grew up, I gave them responsibility in the business and lots of experience."

Each of the sons showed an interest. In 1982, Earl gave the whole business to his sons and retired, "for the first time," as he says with a smile. Just turning fifty, he thought he had it made. He planned to enjoy life with his wife and do all the things he'd been too busy to do. Soon afterward they took a seven-week trip to Alaska. At last they had the kind of life they had dreamed of.

When they returned, he found the business required his attention. He had to straighten up some things. His old work style kicked in again and soon he was driving himself as hard as he had before "retiring."

In the tourist areas of Florida, business is highly seasonal. In the off-season, they all had to supplement their incomes as best they could. Dennis, Earl's middle son, was a paramedic and volunteer fireman. An outgoing guy, he gave himself freely to all kinds of causes and really enjoyed helping people. In August of 1987, at age twenty-seven, he was doing odd jobs to make extra money. On that fateful Saturday afternoon he had some work to do in Bradenton and asked his brother-in-law, Aldo, to come along.

Climbing into his Chevy Suburban, he strapped his three-year-old son, Dwight, in the front seat between himself and Aldo and began the drive over the Manatee Causeway. Traffic was congested. The causeway joins several small islands between Anna

Maria Island and the mainland. He was at the last island before
the mainland when a Pontiac Trans Am approached from the opposite direction going well over the speed limit. At the wheel was
a seventeen-year-old girl drunk and on drugs. She was totally
unaware of the traffic backup just ahead of her. When she finally
saw the brake lights, it was too late. At the last second she veered
to the left into the on-coming traffic and hit the Chevy Suburban
on the driver's front wheel side.

Dennis was killed instantly. Aldo escaped with minor injuries. Three-year-old Dwight was pulled out of the smashed front
window. Both arms and both legs were broken. His spleen was
severely damaged. He suffered a life-threatening spinal chord
injury. He was rushed to nearby Blake Hospital and then air-
lifted to All Children's Hospital in St. Petersburg where Earl met
the helicopter. There they stabilized Dwight. Heroic measures
repaired some of the damage, but he was in bad shape. After four
weeks he was transferred for more specialized treatment at the
Johns Hopkins Medical Center in Baltimore. The final verdict
was severe brain damage and life-long paralysis. He would be a
total invalid and never function normally again. The nightmare
for Dennis's wife and family and for his parents, Earl and Mar-
garet, had just begun.

Words cannot describe the effect that accident had on their
lives. They would never be the same again. As Earl says, "My
whole life turned upside down." Apart from the immense grief
of losing both Dennis and Dwight, there was the huge financial
burden of ongoing care for Dwight. It turned out that there
was no insurance on the Trans Am. It had been removed weeks

before the accident. Earl and Dennis's widow would have to find the funds out of their own insurance and savings. It would be way over a million dollars.

But the most amazing change was the spiritual effect it had on Earl. As a child he had received a basic Christian foundation. Growing up as one of six children in a humble rural area during the Depression, he had learned from his parents the solid values of a good work ethic and the importance of sharing your blessings with others. And they knew about Jesus. His mother was the strong spiritual leader in the home and saw that they never missed church. But Earl remembers it as a rigid fundamentalist church in which Christianity was mostly a matter of keeping the rules.

"You went to church on Sundays not as an option, but because you were told to. As a result I had no personal faith. When I was twelve years old, an evangelist came and I accepted the Lord because it was expected."

In fact, as he grew up he had no real relationship with God. All he knew was work 24/7. The Lord was nowhere in the picture. But Dennis's death changed all that. Some people might have taken their anger out on God, but not Earl.

"I never blamed God for Dennis's death," Earl told me. "God allows things to happen."

So there was no barrier to turning to God.

"That very Sunday I went back to church. There and then I rededicated my life to the Lord. It was something I said in my heart, and for the first time I felt the Lord was part of my life." His new faith opened his heart.

Two or three months after the accident, a lawyer came to speak to the Bible study group which Earl had joined at the church. In the course of his remarks he said to the group, "If you have something or someone in your life that you haven't forgiven, you've got to deal with it. You've got to take it to God."

Earl asked, "Why are you looking at me?"

"I'm not," the man replied with a smile.

Earl couldn't avoid it. He knew it was a word for him about the young woman who had driven the car that killed his son.

"I tried to keep from facing it," he said, "but the next day it was so clear in my heart that I prayed to the Lord, 'If this unforgiveness is going to stand between You and me, then it has to go.'" He determined to go and speak to her.

It was a simple matter to track her down. He had heard she was a quadriplegic and living in the area. He phoned to prepare the way. Yes, she would see him. When Earl knocked on the door, her boyfriend answered and motioned Earl to come in. There she was, propped up in a mechanized wheel chair, only able to operate the control pad in front of her face with her chin. This was the woman who had taken his son's life and made his grandson a permanent invalid.

Going to her, Earl introduced himself and said, "There's something I have to tell you."

Though her body was motionless, tears welled up in her eyes.

Getting down on both knees before her, Earl went on. "The Lord wants me to tell you that He loves you, and that I forgive you and love you too. Will you forgive me?" Now he was in tears.

"Why do you need to be forgiven?" she asked in astonishment. "It's me that needs forgiveness."

"No," he said, "I have hated you and what you did. I ask your forgiveness for that. I don't blame you any more. God loves you and I love you too."

Swallowing hard, he got to his feet, smiled at her warmly, and left. He knew that something vitally important had passed between them.

As he told me that afternoon, "Those things turn such a big corner." Already he was a changed man.

In the years that followed the accident, his human response was to throw himself into work, partly to keep from thinking about the tragedy but also as a way to turn his negatives into positives. There were huge medical bills, and he had to do all he could to build up a trust fund to provide for Dwight's ongoing care. He smiles now about his earlier "retirement" plans. Following the accident, he became more active than ever, starting up a second business in North Carolina to balance the one in Florida. For the next few years his whole focus was on Dwight and how to finance his needs.

Then in 1997, his life took a new direction. A group from Venice, Florida, called Peoples' Relief spoke at his church and asked if anyone would be interested in going on a mission trip to Haiti. The thought of it scared Earl. Never in his whole life had he considered such a thing.

"Not me," he said.

But his wife prodded him gently, "Why don't you go?"

Earl said, "I went to bed to try and forget it, but that night the Lord got me up and wouldn't give me any peace until I said yes."

He was the only one from his church who went with three others from the Venice group. Then the next week, four more from his church joined them for a second week. What they saw was far worse than what they had expected. Everywhere the appalling poverty of the Haitian people and their desperate needs took hold of Earl's heart. He told God he would do whatever God wanted him to do. "If there's a truck to drive, I'll drive it." The answer was not long in coming.

First they met a local pastor named FanFan at Bois Rouge and worked with him and his people to finish a mission house for mission workers to stay in. During the two weeks they were there they hauled in a generator and did the plumbing, electrical wiring, and finishing of the building. Sometimes God's clearest call comes when some human need claims our attention. There, beside the mission house, they saw three hundred children using the church building for school and began talking about building a school alongside the church. After much prayer the group decided to undertake this project. Over the next two years Earl's group and the Peoples' Relief group in partnership with the local Haitian church men built a 50- by 100-foot, eight-room cement school. Financial support came from the home churches of the men in Anna Maria and Venice, Florida, from other Anna Maria, Bradenton, Sarasota, and Venice churches, and from as far away as Indiana. As Earl says, "With the Lord's blessing everything fell into place beautifully, but that is a whole other story."

For a week in September 1999, Earl and the four other members of his group from Island Baptist Church returned with a journalist-photographer team from the Bradenton Herald newspaper to dramatize the plight of the Haitian people.[12] En route home they stayed at an orphanage in Cap Haitien. It was there that an American missionary persuaded them to come as visitors to his nearby church. In the eyes of the local Haitians these men from Florida had a certain aura and fascination, not only because of the resources they brought and the leadership they gave to these building projects, but also because of their faith and personal charisma. At the church service, the pastor asked for a testimony from any of the men from Florida. Earl hung back.

"I wasn't going to be the one. I had my camera running and I was going to stay behind the scenes." But word of his personal tragedy had leaked out. Somehow he was pushed forward and had no choice. Searching for words, Earl spoke as simply as he could in English. The pastor translated into Creole. He told them how the emotion he felt at that moment was of his great loss of Dennis's and Dwight's love. He continued, "You Haitian people don't think you have anything to give. But you have. If each of you as you leave could give me a hug that would say that we love Jesus together, that would be the greatest gift you could give me or any of the others."

Smiling through tears, Earl told me, "Hundreds of people lined up and no one left before hugging me."

---

12. *Bradenton Herald*, 1999: "Flight of Love," December 12; "Practice of Faith," December 13; "Journal Entry," December 13; "Gift of Hope," December 14.

The Haitian children especially were drawn to Earl. Back at the orphanage, he and the others in the relief group took part in the dedication of a gymnasium and basketball court. They were sitting on wooden benches with the rain pouring down outside when a tiny orphan boy emerged from the dormitory nearby and entered the area where the dedication was taking place. He walked up and down the benches, looking each of the people in the eye. When he got to Earl he climbed up on Earl's lap and went to sleep. After the ceremony, Earl carried the sleeping boy back to the nurse and gave her $100. One of the men overheard him tell her with the big smile he constantly wore, "Take good care of my grandson."

To this point Earl had been part of projects that were already in process. Now his real mission was about to begin. When they were finishing the school building at Bois Rouge, Pastor FanFan took their small group to meet Pastor Julio Gilles in the Madeline community some distance away. Pastor Julio showed them the ruins of a burned out shack which had been his church. This was the second time the voodoo witch doctors had tried to eliminate him and his work. Earl and his team began to talk with Julio about building a real building for him and his people.

"Fifteen of us gathered under a nearby tree and prayed for guidance and for God to provide a place for his work there. Little did we know at the time that the place God had in mind would be less than three hundred feet away and that we would build a concrete block church there that would be the spiritual home initially for one hundred and fifty people and it would be fireproof."

Earl came home with a passion and a vision. "Now I had an opportunity to do something for the Lord I'd never done before. Now serving him was more joy than I had ever known."

But they never imagined what they were getting into. Raising the money was only one part of the challenge. Haiti did not have material for roof trusses or the metal sheeting for the roof. It all had to be brought in from Florida. Once the lot was purchased and the plans drawn for the building, Earl and a couple of others returned home and went to Home Depot to look around for what they could take to Haiti for the building.

"We thought we'd spend $200 and ended up buying more than $1000."

This was typical of how they gave the money, raised the funds, and supplied the material for the building, bit by bit, contribution by contribution.

"We stepped out in faith—sometimes little steps—and Jesus always provided for the next step. And when we'd get to Haiti, the people would welcome us with all the warmth of family. The Haitian children especially would swarm around us."

Somehow the children took a special shine to Earl and would follow him, singing and dancing. The other guys began to call him "the Pied Piper." He had never been so happy.

Work teams were organized, and the people of the Madeline village bonded with these men from Florida to lay the foundation and pour the cement blocks.

"You just couldn't control them," Earl said. "The original plan was for a 30 by 50 foot building with eight-foot walls.

Before we knew it the building was 50 by 102 feet with twelve-foot walls."

Funds had to be raised for all of this. Earl would come home from Haiti and go back to his regular TV service business to earn money. Everywhere he went he was a walking ad for the mission work. Out on a service call, strangers would ask him, "How's that work in Haiti going?"

"I'd tell them and they'd put cash or a check in my hand. They wanted to be part of it. Everything we touched turned to gold." That was true of what they raised for the building and the Lord also rewarded them personally.

"I would take a thousand dollars' worth of material down. When I returned and went back to my work, my business would rebound with three thousand dollars' worth of work." In such ways God kept amazing them.

The building started in 2000. As soon as the roof was on, 270 people began worshipping there. The building was finished in 2005.

As part of the dedication, revival meetings were held on Thursday and Friday. "Fifteen hundred people came each night," says Earl, his face beaming, "and a total of seventy-five people gave their hearts to the Lord. Thirteen were baptized." This was typical of how the church grew and how the work was blessed.

The partnership of the Florida men with the Haitian people went very deep. The Haitians affectionately called them "blanc," which loosely translates as "whitey." There were other partners too. In addition to those from Florida, there were individual volunteers who came at their own expense from churches in North and South Carolina, Indiana, Ohio, Pennsylvania, New York, and Illinois to lend a hand. Back home, hundreds of people reached into their pockets to pay for the materials and supplies. Altogether Earl and his four-member team made twenty trips, raised over $30,000, gave another $25,000, helped finish the mission house at Bois Rouge, and built the church and pastor's house at Madeline. The Haitian people supplied most of the labor. The momentum carried forward. Over the next two years, a Canadian group built a school beside the church. Where in 1998 Julio's church had had thirteen members, today six hundred people regularly worship in God's house and over 300 children are being taught about Jesus and receiving a state-regulated education.

No one could have had a more supportive relationship with Julio than Earl had. Clearly it had been Julio's vision from the first. He had been God's man on the scene with the people in need. Often during the difficult years of planning and building, Earl would encourage Julio by email with the phrase "Remember, Pastor, God chose you for such a time as this."

After the dedication, Julio turned it around. "Earl," he said, "He chose you for such a time as this."

Earl felt the truth of that. He could see how for over fifty years he was being prepared to do this work—his business and technical skills, his work ethic, his fundraising among the network of people in the community, and most of all his faith and trust in the Lord.

"For fifty years he had been teaching me. Now it was my turn to give back. Love isn't something we talk about; it's something we do. After fifty years it was my turn to give back. At last,

I had a chance to share what Jesus means to me, what Jesus has done for me."

A key part of that preparation was Earl's faith that grew to trust God in spite of those terrible losses of his son and his grandson. Strangely, his involvement in Haiti would never have happened without Dennis's death. "It changed my life, inside—that I would really want to do something that I should do, like that."

"What was it that inspired you?" I asked.

"Three things: God called me, Dennis's love for others, and God kept opening the doors."

It was a big question and Earl reflected further: "My joy for my Haitian brothers and sisters made my step spring again." It was written all over his face. He genuinely loved these people and rejoiced in their new-found life.

As I looked at him, now knowing his journey since that terrible tragedy, I just shook my head in wonder. Here was this man, his six-foot, three-inch frame bent and humbled by the stroke, needing the support of his cane and walker, having every worldly reason to be bitter and resentful, yet with the most glorious smile on his face … for joy!

It was his final comment, though, that touched me most deeply:

"There I was with my broken heart and God was asking, 'Do you want to make this a good experience or a bad one?'"

"Don't Cry. Rejoice!"

The greatest evidence of God in some people's lives is not in what happens to them but in what they do with what happens to them. Not enough had happened in John's life to make God real to him until he was fifty-three. That's when his wife gave him an ultimatum.

Up to then he'd managed okay, so he thought. The third of eight children born to a poor family in rural New Jersey in the early 1920s, he had a "wonderful childhood." There in the ridge country, it was a boy's paradise—fields and woods, animals and berries of all kinds—and camp in the summer. After high school he did various jobs through the lean years and finally was working for General Electric when the war came. In 1943 he joined the regular navy and served for six years. He went from camp to camp and then served on a destroyer escort but never went to a battle area. He was assigned to a ship but didn't see action. His ship was ready for the invasion of Japan when the Japanese surrendered. He was there in the harbor when General MacArthur signed the armistice.

After the war he met and married May and shipped to Saipan where he was in charge of the mess for fourteen months. Returning to California, he worked in various jobs in restaurants and construction. They had two children, a boy and a girl. It was the big money in construction that got him in trouble. Gambling, mostly, and women. But he figured he could get away with it. For years he did. All through those years May and their daughter would pray for him. She would beg him to go to church with her and the family. He refused. She pleaded with him to give up his gambling that was bleeding them financially. But he would just lie about it. She never knew how much he actually made. Finally, his reckless lifestyle was too much for her. That's when she gave him the ultimatum.

"Either you give me your check when you come out of work or I go in there and get it from the boss myself."

John knew the jig was up. He handed over his paycheck and she gave him an allowance. From then on she managed the money.

But John knew he'd come to a moment of truth. If he kept on his old ways, he would lose his wife and family. He began to think of what he'd done. It wasn't pretty. He knew he was to blame and that he needed help.

Lying awake one night he prayed to God. "I don't know much about you," he said. "But I want you to come into my life and help me walk the walk." His body began to shake violently, and he couldn't stop it. It was frightening.

"Then," as he told me later, "a wonderful peace came over me and I knew He was in my life."

The first thing John did was throw out what cigarettes and booze he had. Then he just stopped gambling, stopped lying, and broke off the wrong relationships.

"I started to pick up the Bible regularly. Nobody was there to help me understand. Nobody taught me. I just read the Bible. That's how I came to know that Jesus took care of every lousy sin I'd ever done. Incredible!"

May noticed a change in John. For one thing he came to her and said, "I'm going to go to church with you." And he did. In time she knew that he'd stopped gambling and womanizing, but trust was slow to come. Hearing of his faith commitment was a positive.

"It helped when I realized that he'd given his heart to the Lord. After that I just turned him over to God. 'It's up to You,' I said."

How hard was it for John? "It was no problem stopping," he told me. "I just lost complete interest in it. When my racetrack buddies would ask, I'd just say, 'I'm sorry, I've quit.'" Slowly he and May rebuilt their marriage and are now celebrating sixty-three years.

For the last twenty years John has been visiting men in jail on a weekly basis. He knows the kinds of things we humans do in our sinful natures and wants them to know the One who has helped him so much.

"I've talked to hundreds and hundreds of men in jail and I've never met one who was not sorry for what he had done. The trouble is that not one of us can deal with our Adamic nature without the help of the Holy Spirit."

He pulled out a thick binder full of stories of men's lives and of letters he had received from them. He read me one from a man he had visited twenty years before, telling how his life had been guided and blessed ever since that day when he had committed his life to Christ with John.

The biggest challenge, though, has been a personal one. Three years ago their daughter, Candy, was diagnosed with

ovarian cancer. She had been married for many years but because
of a rare medical condition could not have children. For over
thirty years she had devoted herself to special education in the
school system. She was a respected and greatly loved teacher. But
now her very life was threatened.

Chemotherapy was undertaken at once and by January 2008,
her doctors reported that no evidence of cancer remained. She
went on a vacation to celebrate and visited family and friends in
high spirits. But by the end of April symptoms returned and a
secondary cancer was found in her stomach and bowel. Intensive
radiation followed, but by October the doctors could offer no
hope. They sent her home from the hospital and recommended
that she be moved into a hospice. She phoned her father to tell
him. For a long time John had denied the possibility, but now he
could no longer avoid it: she was going to die.

In protest, he blurted out on the phone, "I'm the head of
this family. I should go first."

Calmly but firmly she answered him. "It's not up to you. It's
up to the Lord."

At the hospice, her devoted husband sat by her side as friends
and acquaintances came to visit. Invariably she would focus on
their needs and send them out with a prayer for their blessing.
From her sickbed she even organized a party to honor her mother. Thirty-two women attended. It seemed that the whole world
loved Candy and was praying for her.

A few weeks before she died, she contacted her parents: "I
want you to come up while I'm still ambulatory and I've got my
senses. We can have a nice visit for four days."

When they came, she told them, "I'm going to die. I've already made arrangements for my service, the hymns and Scripture readings, even what the preacher is going to say."

Tears flooded every eye. They prayed. Then she said, "Don't cry. Rejoice! I'm going home."

Candy had come to terms with it. "Some of us do not get well," she said. "God has taught me so much since I got cancer that I would not have known otherwise. Dad, I'm going to be there to greet you!" Her faith and theirs took the sting of death away. It was seeing her suffer that was breaking their hearts. They could rejoice once that was past. As John said, "At my age you know you don't have a long time. It's just the snap of a finger. We're going for eternity. I think of all the believers who will be there. I know it will be a joyful place." What a response!

Two weeks before Candy died, John and May's church received the following letter with the heading "A special thank you from the daughter of John and May Kamin." It read:

To all who have prayed for me: Words cannot express how grateful I am for all of your prayers and loving support during my journey. I am peaceful and even joyful as I see the finish line ahead, and anticipate seeing our Lord face to face! I also look forward to seeing each and every one of you in Heaven to thank you in person for the love of Christ poured out to me and my family. God bless you richly as you continue the most important and powerful labor of prayer. I am eternally grateful.

Love, Candy

She died on December 6. Everything went according to the arrangements Candy had made. There was a triumphant celebration of her life and her faith. John and May were swept up in the outpouring of love, even from strangers. Afterward, they returned to their home in Florida to pick up their lives again.

Only a few days later it was John's day to visit the jail. He told his visiting partner he didn't feel up to going that day. The grief had drained him of energy.

His friend persisted: "John, I think you ought to come."

"So I went," he says. "We stood in the room where we were used to having fifteen come for our meeting. There were ten chairs but no men. No one had come. Something was wrong. I asked the guard, 'Can you put out five more chairs?'" The guard looked at him strangely but did as he had been asked.

"So we had fifteen chairs. Then, slowly, the men started to come in until all the chairs were filled. I preached and played my harmonica and gave an invitation. Eight guys came forward to receive Christ."

Then he explained, "I think the delay was so the Holy Spirit could show me, 'It's not you, John. It's Me.'" That pretty well explains everything.

Vietnamese Mite

Jim Hatton looked out over the twenty young Vietnamese men and women sitting in his classroom there in Phnom Penh, Cambodia. They ranged in age from eighteen to thirty, but to Jim they looked younger—too young for the daunting task they had undertaken. They had come from all across North and South Vietnam, some for over one thousand kilometers, to attend the twelve-week intensive Discipleship Training School (DTS) run by Youth With A Mission.[13] Afterward they would return to do Christian ministry in their local villages.

Jim was there to lead a one-week course on family relationships with a focus on healing past hurts. It was 2007. Many of the parents and grandparents of those students had suffered traumas and atrocities during the Vietnam War whose effects had trickled down into their own young lives. In addition, Jim knew from his ministry to families across East Asia and the Pacific Rim that many of those students had likely experienced abuse of one sort or another due to the cultural biases of male dominance and hierarchical authority. Much of his work focused on abusive and absent fathers and dysfunctional families. Yet in his twenty-three years of ministry in that area he had never encountered a more shocking or victorious story than he was to hear that day.

When the time came for ministry to individual class members, Rene★, a diminutive young woman of nineteen, was the first to come forward for prayer. He learned later that she came

---

13. YWAM is a Christian organization with workers in every country in the world.

from a minority tribe in the mountains of southern Vietnam. She had been selected to play for the national women's soccer team but chose to come to the DTS instead. With Jim and the interpreter, she prayed that God would help her forgive her father for his abuse and that she would be healed of the resentment and fear that she felt. Jim prayed with her. She overflowed with tears when he spoke to her of the Heavenly Father's love for her and when he assured her that God was with her. At the end she smiled warmly and thanked Jim. He then went on to another student.

At noon, the leader mentioned that two of the students had requested individual consultations with Jim. One of the two was Rene. She began by explaining how hard it was to forgive her father, who was a violent alcoholic. Jim could see the scar on her right forearm; and, parting her thick hair, she revealed a fifteen-centimeter scar on top of her head. In drunken rages her father had thrown knives at her and her younger brother and sister. All three had ended up in the hospital, requiring dozens of stitches. This kind of abuse was a regular occurrence until Rene was eight years old. That was when her mother became seriously ill and had to be taken to the hospital.

Without warning her father gathered up his wife and left for the hospital in a distant city. He did not tell the three children where he was going or how long he would be gone. That is highly unusual. Generally, Vietnamese families are tightly knit. But Rene's parents left them without any instruction, without any money, without even an embrace or a goodbye. There was no extended family support. She was eight years old and suddenly in total charge of her young brother and sister. There was little food in the house. Days passed. The food ran out. Nobody came to see how the children were doing. Rene's father was so hated by the whole community that they did not care about his children either.

Rene and her siblings were famished. As a young girl, Rene had gone with her father to the stream to pan for gold. She had watched and learned and soon became his helper, finding the little flecks of gold in the sand. Without any food or means to obtain it, Rene picked up her father's tools and pan and went to the stream. She set about panning and was successful. As she had gone into town with her father when he exchanged the gold for currency, she knew where to go and how this worked. It became a routine. Early in the day she would pan a little gold, go to town, sell it, visit the markets, and buy food.

One day when she was away panning for gold, people came and took all the furnishings from the house. Later she learned that her mother had required prolonged medical treatment and her father had to sell everything to pay the hospital bills. He had incurred other debts as well and settled the accounts by telling creditors to go and get the furniture. Rene and her siblings were now alone in their empty house with not even a mat to sleep on, no pots or pans to cook or wash in. Everything was taken and she was powerless to do anything about it. By now she was nine. It was a whole year after her parents had left. In telling these experiences to Jim there were no tears or signs of resentment. But tears flowed freely when Jim spoke words of encouragement—of God's love for her and of her eternal worth to Him.

She continued with her story. Now Rene needed more gold in order to replace the cooking utensils and sleeping mats.

She worked very hard, panning for gold as well as managing the household and caring for her brother and sister. By the grace of God she was increasingly successful in finding gold. This freed enough time for her to begin the work of clearing a patch of ground to begin to sow crops of basic vegetables. She used a machete to cut down the bamboo and a mattock to dig the roots out—a difficult task even for a strong man to do.

Rene wasn't sure exactly how long her parents were absent. She could barely read and had no access to any means of tracking the date. All she knew was that the wet and dry seasons passed several times. It must have been two to three years. Her mother survived and she returned with her husband. He had not changed. He and his wife treated their absence as if it were only a matter of days. There were no apologies from either father or mother; they just started to relate to their children again as if nothing unusual had happened.

Rene's father continued to drink; but now his abuse was only verbal and emotional, not physical. However, about four years after his return, he had a radical conversion to Jesus and was instantly delivered from his alcoholism. He began to help around the house. He began to show more care for his wife and children. Rene, as a bright young teenager now, went to high school. She did well in her studies and excelled in sports.

Then, the year before Rene came to the DTS, her father died suddenly. Her mother, still weakened from her earlier sickness, was left alone to care for her still-growing children. Of course, Rene was still there to help, and things worked out for the best.

After she had poured out her story to Jim, Rene experienced a cathartic release from bitterness, hatred, and resentment through prayer and the laying on of hands. The change was dramatic. Raising her hands, she cried out in her own language, "I'm free of this! I'm free of this!" She had come in heavily weighed down. She left radiant and smiling. In the next few days she shared all of this with the whole DTS and continued to grow in her freedom. At the end of the week, as Jim was leaving, she came to him and embraced him warmly. "I love you," she said. "Thank you!"

The Lord's blessing continued. As she went on to complete the DTS, Rene had a sense that God wanted her to go back to her village and to open an orphanage for the numerous children living on the streets. But how? Earlier, her village, recognizing her achievement in caring for her siblings and her determination to overcome her parents' abandonment, had given her the piece of land she had cleared and farmed. By the time her parents had returned, it was about half a hectare.[14] Now she knew that on that land she would build her orphanage. She was only nineteen. Her youth had never held her back before, and it would not hold her back now.

As Jim reflected on the brief week he had spent there, Rene's story made the deepest impression on him. He knew that he had had the extraordinary privilege to meet, talk, and pray with an incredible young woman. She had shown almost superhuman power in overcoming adversity. He also knew that she had received from God something that she could not give herself—inner freedom and the beginning of the healing of her childhood wounds.

---

14. One hectare equals 2.47105 acres.

WAITING

Waiting is a frustration for most of us. Whether it is sitting in traffic or standing in line at the checkout, it can be a major irritant in our busy lives. We have an agenda and any delay seems a waste.

This kind of waiting, though, is secondary to the more profound obstacles to our progress in life—being an unemployed person waiting for a job or an urgent patient waiting for an organ donor or a childless couple waiting to get pregnant. These delays and frustrations test us at the deepest level.

There are benefits, however, to be found in waiting. Next to suffering, it can be one of the best teachers of maturity and spiritual discipline. Waiting requires a reshuffling of our priorities and attitudes. It breaks the illusion that we can control life. In forcing us to accept a timetable contrary to our wishes, it teaches us patience and humility. Best of all, it acquaints us with God through His seeming absence by teaching us faith. "Now faith is the substance of things hoped for, the evidence of things not seen" (Hebrews 11:1 NKJV).

Be Still And Know

"Why would God promise to take care of me and then pull the plug?" Seated opposite me in the restaurant, my friend John was telling me how his faith had been tested.

In March 1999, he'd had a powerful dream in which God told him everything was going to be all right and instructed him, "Be still, and know that I am God." Less than a month later, the bank he served as Executive Vice President and Chief Financial Officer announced it would be closing down in October. He'd been with them for fifteen years and had a great track record. So in May, when a U.S. financial company, a subsidiary of the same bank he served, expressed an interest in purchasing the Canadian operation and told him they would offer him the CFO position, he thought that was what God had meant. What "impeccable timing" God had.

John had always had a personal faith in God's goodness. Born to devout Methodist Christians in Malaysia, he had been raised in the church. Through his parents' sacrifice and his own hard work and spiritual discipline, John had gone to the UK, received a first-class education, and qualified as a chartered accountant. He immigrated to Canada in 1981, after receiving a job offer.

John had experienced one gracious blessing after another. He met his wife while he was in the UK, married, and had two healthy, gifted children. Employers sought him out. Then he was offered the job at the bank in Canada and it had been upward from there. They owned their own home and were well on the way to providing university education for their children. Now, after fifteen years, this contingent offer of a secure position in the new bank seemed like just one more example of God's goodness to John.

But then the undreamed of happened. In August the deal fell through. The bank he worked with was sold to a Canadian bank instead. They had no need of John and he was let go at the end of December with a severance package. He was devastated.

"In my sorrow and darkest hour I fell on my knees and asked why God would allow something like this to happen. I would be out of a job for the first time in my life. What would I do? I could not understand why God would put me on a pedestal and then let me fall."

At that moment he saw that up until then he'd had a very comfortable faith. It had never really been tested.

He asked himself, "Now am I going to trust God completely?"

In September God spoke to him again in his sleep: "Be still, and know that I am God."

He had never had to look for a job before. Was God telling him to do nothing and simply trust Him? This was the first test of his faith: would he trust God's guidance to "be still" when what seemed like sure blessings had gone wrong? His wife urged him to wait and see how God would provide.

The second test was of his eagerness to find his own human solutions. In the weeks that followed, several chance meetings with Christian men involved in executive recruitment raised his hopes that there might be something there for him. One of these friends was starting a company and was looking for a CFO but couldn't afford to pay John anything. John volunteered to help him get started. He would benefit from the fellowship and thought that if the company grew there might be an opportunity for him. As it turned out, no job came of this.

A third test of his faith came when he heard that the deal with the Canadian bank had been halted. He thought perhaps it would open the way for the U.S. affiliate to purchase the bank after all and give him a job. But this did not happen and his hopes were dashed. At that point all his human willing and wishing gave way.

"I went down on my knees," he said, "and completely surrendered everything to Jesus. I told Him I would accept whatever He did."

A period of listening and waiting followed in which John received repeated assurances through the preaching and praise ministries of his church and on TV. He asked for and received prayer support from his church fellowship and from a network of Christian friends. He was invited to join a weekly Bible study with four other men. Still obedient to the instruction to be still and trust God, John did not seek work himself but volunteered to help his friend in his business, beginning in January.

A fourth test came in January when he thought he should not renew his tithe offering since he was unemployed. He was still in the severance period, however, and his wife advised him to continue tithing since the Lord had blessed him financially. When he prayed about it, God spoke to his heart and told him to give more than he had been giving when he was working. With that came the assurance that God would open the floodgates and bless him even more. John signed the check with the amount God placed in his heart. Still there were no job offers.

The fifth and final test was more personal and crushing. Word came that his mother had died in Malaysia. They begged him to come home to be with the family. To bring his whole family home to Malaysia would be expensive and he was still without a job. Why does God allow so many bad things to happen all at the same time? he thought.

In that darkest hour God reminded him again: "Be still, and know that I am God."

God is still God, he assured himself. Faithfully, he took his wife and daughter and flew home to comfort his father and sister and their relatives—at a cost of over $7,000.

Returning to Canada in March, he resolved to continue to volunteer in his friend's business development. If that were not successful, he would trust God to find him the right job. It was then that his faith was rewarded. A phone call from a distant acquaintance asked if he would be interested in a position as CFO with a U.S. company expanding in Canada, exactly the same situation he had first been offered. Three weeks later he was interviewed and was hired to start immediately. He would be paid in U.S. dollars and his salary would be more than he had been making before. Together with the signing bonus, it was far beyond the amount on which he had been tithing.

"At that moment," says John, "the words 'be still, and know that I am God' were fulfilled."

At the end of the year he reflected on his finances and realized that the total severance amount was intact: all of his costs during the unemployment time including the increased tithe and the trip to Malaysia had been paid out of savings! The job God had given him was better pay and very similar to the job he had before. This was something which John had hoped and prayed for.

But the monetary benefits were superficial compared with the spiritual growth that occurred in him. Why does God promise and then pull the plug? Now he was ready to form a kind of answer: "God used this time of trials and tribulations to show me that He is a faithful and loving God Who cares about the problems and lives of his children if only we would trust Him and surrender our lives to Him."

Looking back, John realized that for a long time he had been drifting away from God. He had been too comfortable. "I thought I had it made, that God was just an option."

Now he had come to trust God more completely. "I have come to know Him. I hear God's voice so much clearer now. It took a crisis. But God is always faithful to those who believe in Him." Psalm 46:10, "Be still, and know that I am God," has become an anchor in John's life.

God Keeps A Promise

Barry and Beth Cleave had decided to sell their auto shop and garage. It was located in a small village in Ontario. Over the

Along Comes God

Order Form

(Canada)

<u>Special Offer</u>:

Payment <u>only</u> by <u>cheque</u> or <u>money order</u>.

Or email money transfer to <u>georgeslater@sympatico.ca</u>

1 book: $13.99 plus $.4.95 Shipping & Handling
2-4 copies to one address: $12.99 each, plus $9.75 S&H
5-8 copies to one address: $11.99 each, plus $14.95 S&H
10 copies to one address: $11.99 each, <u>FREE</u> S&H

For <u>credit card</u> price and purchase go to <u>www.alongcomesgod.com</u>

For <u>Special Offer</u>, order below by circling desired Quantity and Total:

Quantity	Unit Price	Cost	S&H	Total
1	$13.99	$ 13.99	$4.95	$18.94
2	12.99	25.98	9.75	35.73
3	"	38.97	"	48.72
4	"	51.96	"	61.71
5	11.99	59.95	14.95	74.90
6	"	71.94	"	86.89
7	"	83.93	"	98.88
8	"	95.92	"	110.87
10	11.99	119.90	FREE	119.90

No GST/HST

Name (please print)..

Mailing Address...

.... Postal Code ....

Phone .... Email ....

Cheque ......   Money Order .... enclosed.   Amount $...............

Make payable to "George R. Slater". Please mail to: George Slater

16815 St. Andrew's Rd.

Inquiries: <u>georgeslater@sympatico.ca</u>   Caledon, ON L7C 2S4

eight years since opening, Barry had built up the business, had earned a solid reputation for dependable service, and was making a good living. But, at forty-five with his family raised, he wanted a change. So they listed the property with real estate and waited. Nothing. Not a call. They let the listing expire and recommitted to the work, but they still wanted to sell.

Both he and Beth had a personal faith in Christ and attended church and a small mid-week group for prayer and Bible study. Around the time the listing expired, they were meeting with this group and happened to mention that there had been no interest in the property and that they had taken it off the market.

Tom, one of the group members, spoke up with special authority: "The Lord will look after things. When it is the right time to sell, a stranger will come to the shop and ask if it is for sale. You will see him coming and you will know he is the buyer."

The prophecy made a deep impression on Barry and Beth.

"Every time we'd start to think about selling," Beth said, "I'd remember that that word of prophecy had been given. I couldn't get that word out of my mind. If we listed, it would seem that we would be taking these things into our own hands." Barry kept on working.

Ten years passed, when one day he received a very attractive offer of a job some distance away. It was right in his area of expertise—auto and heavy equipment technician. The benefits and salary were good and all the moving costs would be covered. He and Beth were tempted to accept. They listed the shop again, this time for over two years with three different real estate companies. Absolutely nothing. They finally let the listing expire. He gave up any hope of accepting any other job and kept on working. The business prospered.

Then, just four days before Christmas 2004, a man pulled up in front of the shop. He came in and walked around. He didn't speak but just looked around. Finally he asked about the building beside the garage, which was also part of Barry's shop. Barry said it was a warehouse.

"Could I see it?" asked the stranger.

"Yes," was Barry's response.

He looked in the warehouse. "This would be perfect." They went back into the garage where it was warm.

"I understand this might be for sale," the man began.

"I guess anything's for sale," replied Barry.

"Could you name a figure?" the man asked.

"Yes, I could." As Barry explained later, "I figured he would need the garage, the warehouse, the property, and the equipment. So I gave him a price to include all of that."

"I couldn't pay that much," the man countered.

"Then tell me how much you could pay." Barry says, "When he told me, it wasn't much lower than what I had asked. So I said, 'You know, I think I could live with that!' Then we shook hands to make the deal."

"Okay. I'll have an offer in writing in a couple of days."

"Hold on," said Barry. "I'll have to share this with Beth, my wife; she's a part owner." Barry talked with Beth and they agreed to accept the stranger's offer.

"I phoned him the same day and told him it was a go. He said, 'I'll bring you a written offer.' I told him, 'Bring it in January.'"

Then Barry asked him, "Now what equipment do you want?"

He said, "Nothing. I just want the buildings."

Barry told him all that came for the same price—the building, heating, machines, and a hoist. The man didn't want the hoist or the machinery.

"When Barry came and told me," Beth reminisced, "I just had a sense of real excitement in my spirit. When we look back, it's like we never had to do anything. It happened exactly as it had been foretold."

For Barry also it was surely the Lord's doing. "There's no way this could have happened otherwise. So smooth, so easy."

Why had the stranger come? Barry thinks that he may have inquired of a mechanic who lived in the subdivision about warehouse space and the mechanic may have said, "Try the guy in the garage; he might want to sell."

"That was all," Barry says. "There was no real estate involved, no advertising, no plan or expectation."

It turned out the stranger only wanted the buildings for warehouse storage, so when they got the offer in January Barry began to sell off the tools and equipment. He had a sale in May.

"Just a little bit of an ad," said Barry. "The rest was word of mouth. The phone kept ringing. Everything sold. At good prices! Some guys drove off with truckloads."

The deal closed on June 30, 2005. Barry and Beth settled back into their home in the village for a well-deserved retirement. It was twenty years since they had been given the prophecy: "The Lord will look after things. When it is the right time to sell, a stranger will come...."

For Barry and Beth it was the right time. For years she had kept the books and done all the paper work. Barry was tired and in those last months had difficulty staying focused. They were both ready.

"The garage was getting to the point of needing painting and fixing," Barry explained. "We didn't realize how ready we were to quit until we got the offer."

Beth was even more enthusiastic: "Give God the glory! We're just so thankful."

Yes, the Lord did look after things, just as they had been told. The length of time did not bother Barry and Beth. To them it was right in every way. By means of the prophecy, they were given the faith to wait.

Mrs. B. And The Ferryboat Captain

Sometimes a word of truth comes in a most unexpected way. In this case it was through a widow who may have thought that her usefulness was over.

Mrs. B. lived alone in a small town east of Montreal. She and her husband had lived in the same modest house there for many years. After his death she continued in those familiar surroundings and in that community where she felt the support of friends and neighbors. But she was lonely and decided to take in a boarder.

So it was that, one summer in the late 1950s, I came to board at her house. As a single theological student doing my summer internship, I had been assigned to a tiny, newly formed congregation in that town. Surveying the community and visiting the people kept me quite busy. However, over meals, I learned details of her life and family and of her many interests. She would often speak of her late husband and recall memories of their lives together. They loved to travel by car and in his retirement they had visited different parts of Canada. Prince Edward Island had been high on their "must see" list. In relating the many rich experiences of that trip, she told me the following vignette which has remained vividly in my mind all these years.

It was long before the bridge connecting PEI to the mainland was built. Today Confederation Bridge spans the eight miles of ocean, and vehicles easily make the journey in less than fifteen minutes. In those days, however, those traveling to and from the island were dependent on one or other of two ferries. Knowing the timetable and making allowance for the line-ups at various seasons of the year was important. Mrs. B. and her husband had spent most of the day exploring the hamlets along the shores of the Bay of Fundy and Chignecto Bay in New Brunswick and observing the huge tides. So they had let time slip away and were behind schedule making their way to the ferry.

It was nearly dark when they came to the last few miles of lowlands which lie along the shore of Northumberland Strait. The timetable showed that the last ferry would leave soon and they must use every minute to catch it. Her husband pressed heavier on the accelerator and the car sped over the winding road. But it was unfamiliar to them and he didn't want to take too many chances.

Then the unexpected. Rounding a bend, they came face to face with a railroad crossing and a freight train lumbering slowly across. Her husband brought the car to an abrupt halt and sighed. Now they would almost certainly miss the ferry. He looked at his watch and shook his head. Only a few minutes left. Still miles to go.

When the last car finally rumbled past, he was across the tracks in a shot. He went as fast as the narrow road permitted. At least there were no other cars. Traveling through the darkness over the rolling countryside, they thought they caught sight of lights in the far distance. Then from the next hilltop, they were sure. It was the mast lights of a boat. They pressed for even more speed. Was the boat still there? It was now past the time. As they rounded the last bend, they saw the ferry. Yes. It was still docked.

Guiding the car quickly up the ramp, her husband made a soft landing on the boat deck and brought the car to a full stop beside the wheelhouse. He breathed a huge sigh of relief. "We made it!"

A crewmember standing nearby, hearing this, shot back, "You made it? We saw your lights coming. The Capt'n's been waiting for you."

Whenever I get too focused on my part in an undertaking or am tempted to think that success all depends on me, I recall the lesson of Mrs. B.'s story: "The Capt'n's been waiting for you."

AFTERWORD

The first response to such miraculous stories is surely wonder. These are regular people who had extraordinary things happen in their lives. Reading their experiences, we are introduced to a dimension of life some of us may never have known before—a world of faith where God is in charge and miracles happen. It causes us to take another look at our own lives and the world around us and to wonder. Could God be at work blessing us and we are not aware? Is God present but we have not acknowledged Him or reached out in faith or asked for help? Have we been neglecting the greatest resource in the world? We can be grateful to these people for reporting what happened and for opening their personal lives as an inspiration to others. Their stories show that God is real in the here and now. The wonder of it invites us to bring an attitude of faith and expectancy to every day.

At the same time, such a triumphant view of life could appear to be overly optimistic and in need of balance. Well and good to report, along comes God; but what of the times when God does not come along, or does not appear to come along? When prayers are unanswered or when evil seems to triumph? When miracles don't happen and life is flat, empty, and boring? Without acknowledging the harsh realities also present in ordinary life, these stories of faith being fulfilled could seem unrealistic and out of touch.

Certainly, hearing of God's kindly interventions raises profound questions. Foremost among them is the paradox of good and evil, often called the problem of suffering: If God is credited with the good things, is God also responsible for the bad things? And if God is all-powerful, is it not immoral to allow bad things to happen? The conflict is heightened when, in some of the stories, selfish or even trivial prayers are answered, while we know of prayers for more worthy human needs that go unanswered. It raises the larger problem of favoritism: why some prayers are answered and others are not. And what role does faith play in favorable outcomes? Then there is the question of special revelation: Is God's power more available to those who call on the name of Christ? Finally, there is the problem of miracles. Does God break the laws of nature? Also, is God only known in the exceptional things that we can't explain naturally?

These are complex issues, certainly beyond the scope of this collection of stories.

I mention them to recognize the honest doubts and questions of those whose experiences or conclusions may be different from those presented here. We must acknowledge as well that the presence of evil is a mystery we cannot explain, just as we do not understand God's timing and the method of answering prayers or performing miracles.

In fairness, nothing in these stories of goodness denies that all of us stand on the same muddy earth when it comes to the challenges and uncertainties of life. Hardship is real and evil a perplexity that faith in God must answer. In fact, many of those whose stories are told here endured severe suffering and tragic circumstances. So this book is not written out of a high spirit of elite faith or superior achievement. It does, however, recognize miracles when they happen. If there has been a victory of faith, let God's grace be acknowledged. If there has been a healing, a vision, or a saving moment, let us credit God's mercy. As the blind man whom Jesus healed said, "One thing I know: that though I was blind, now I see" (John 9:25 NKJV). Equally, when tragedy and natural disasters happen, let us acknowledge the challenge this creates for faith in God's goodness.

Facing life with faith does not remove the reality of suffering and hardship. The cross of Christ is the most compelling evidence of that. There on the cross God's own Son becomes a victim, and His anguished cry, "My God, my God, why have you forsaken me?" (Matthew 27:46 NKJV) puts the question of God's goodness in the starkest terms. What begins as the paradox of good and evil leads on to the mystery of sacrificial love and the suffering of God.

In this world the elements of good and evil are so mixed that there is always ambiguity. It seems for every positive we can cite a negative. With the world as it is, we can only speak of God in terms of mystery and contradiction. So we know God by faith in the midst of a world of doubt.

Faith is like a secret decoding device. Through the mists of contradiction it makes out the shape of the divine presence and purpose. Faith also permits us to value the things of God more highly than the things that seem to deny God—so that a few stories of goodness breaking out, or of prayer being answered, have a disproportionate effect to inspire and carry us forward. With faith, even what is contrary or difficult becomes acceptable and good.

250

ALONG COMES GOD

One of Jesus' stories illustrates this: "The kingdom of heaven is like treasure hidden in a field, which a man found and hid; and for joy over it he goes and sells all that he has and buys that field" (Matthew 13:44 NKJV). The mundane world can be as empty as a field until we discover God's treasure. Miracle stories give us a reason for joy that makes the whole of life, difficulties and all, worthwhile.

In conclusion, here are some guidelines for living gleaned from these stories:

1. There is always hope. You can never tell when a miracle might happen. We are not in control. No one knows what surprising change might come tomorrow to create a new future.

2. God may be waiting for us to open our eyes. Divine guidance might be right in front of us, but we aren't aware, expectant, or ready. God may be offering us miracles that need only our faith, cooperation, or obedience to happen.

3. What you believe makes a difference. Most, if not all, of the people in these stories are people of faith. Many of them are Christians or became Christians as a result of their experience. Faith knows that God holds the mystery together and will fulfill it.

4. Prayer aligns us with great power and wisdom. But it is God's wisdom, not ours, and so we must learn to wait or to ask differently (see James 4:3) or to accept no as an answer. Prayer is not magic but flows from a relationship with God.

5. We do not know whether an event is good or bad until we see its outcome, and that outcome may take a long time to be revealed. Let us wait patiently for God. Sometimes, in

trying circumstances, we are given the opportunity to make the outcome better than when we began. Often God's best work is done through the response we make to tragedy and difficulty.

6. There is a contagion to good things. The October 2010 rescue of the Chilean miners is a case in point. When the last miner, Luis Urzua, the underground supervisor, was brought safely to the surface, the Chilean president, Sebastian Pinera, said to him, "You are not the same, and the country is not the same after this. You were an inspiration."[15] Good has the power to transform life. Stories of divine and human goodness inspire us to make the world a better place.

7. Human life is more than human. When people are able to forgive their enemies, to love and not hate, to postpone reward, and to give themselves up for others—as some do in these stories—we see a kind of supernatural or transformed humanity (see 2 Corinthians 5:15–17). It leads us to believe that in every person there are divine qualities and capabilities waiting to be activated by faith and empowered by the Holy Spirit. No longer do we regard anyone, even ourselves, from a merely human point of view.

---

15. AOLnews.com, October 14, 2010.

VISIT THE AUTHOR'S WEBSITE:
www.alongcamegod.com

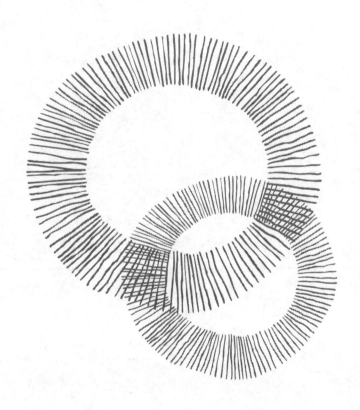